MW01170246

JAKE MADISON

SPOTTED TURTLE

First published by Jake Madison 2025

Copyright © 2025 by Jake Madison

All rights reserved. No part of this publication may be reproduced, stored or transmitted in any form or by any means, electronic, mechanical, photocopying, recording, scanning, or otherwise without written permission from the publisher. It is illegal to copy this book, post it to a website, or distribute it by any other means without permission.

First edition

This book was professionally typeset on Reedsy.
Find out more at reedsy.com

Contents

Chapter 1

WHAT ARE SPOTTED TURTLES?

Spotted turtles, scientifically known as Clemmys guttata, are small freshwater turtles easily identified by the bright yellow or orange spots on their dark shells. These spots are not just for looks—they help the turtles blend into their natural surroundings, acting as a form of camouflage. Adult spotted turtles are quite small compared to other turtles, typically growing to about 3.5 to 5 inches (9 to 12 centimeters) in length.

These turtles are semi-aquatic, meaning they split their time between water and land. They are curious by nature and move quite slowly, which makes them enjoyable to observe for turtle enthusiasts. Spotted turtles can live a long time, often surviving for several decades. In captivity, with the right care, some can live to be 50 years old or even older.

Unfortunately, spotted turtles face many challenges in the wild. They are considered a species of concern in many areas due to threats like habitat destruction, illegal collection for the pet trade, and other human activities. Their habitats, such as wetlands, ponds, and marshes, are often drained or polluted, leaving them with fewer places to live and thrive. This makes it especially important to understand these turtles and their needs, both for those interested in their conservation and for people who want to keep them as pets responsibly.

Keeping a spotted turtle as a pet requires a good understanding of their behavior and care. Since they are semi-aquatic, they need a habitat that includes both water for swimming and land where they can bask and rest. The water should be clean and of the right temperature, and the land area should have places where the turtles can hide and feel safe. Feeding them a balanced diet is also important. Spotted turtles eat a variety of foods, including insects, worms, and some plant material. Providing them with the right nutrition is key to keeping them healthy and helping them live a long life.

In addition to their physical needs, spotted turtles are known for their calm and curious personalities, which makes them interesting pets. They are not fast or aggressive, and they often seem to enjoy exploring their surroundings. However, they are best suited for experienced turtle keepers who understand their specific requirements. Beginners may find it challenging to provide the right environment and care for these turtles.

Spotted turtles are more than just cute and fascinating animals—they are an important part of their ecosystems. In the wild, they help maintain the balance of their habitats by eating a mix of plants and small animals, which keeps populations in check. Protecting them is not only important for the species but also for the health of the ecosystems they are part of.

Conservation efforts are essential for ensuring the future of spotted turtles. Many organizations work to protect their habitats and educate people about the dangers they face. Simple actions like preserving wetlands, avoiding pollution, and not taking turtles from the wild can make a big difference. If you see a spotted turtle in the wild, it is best to leave it alone and appreciate it in its natural environment.

For those who wish to keep spotted turtles as pets, it is important to acquire them from reputable sources that follow legal and ethical guidelines. Wild turtles should never be taken from their habitats, as this can harm local populations. Instead, look for breeders who specialize in captive-raised spotted turtles. This not only supports conservation efforts but also ensures that you are starting with a healthy turtle that is accustomed to living in captivity.

NATURAL HABITAT AND GEOGRAPHIC RANGE

Spotted turtles are native to North America and can be found in the eastern United States and parts of southern Canada. They live in areas stretching from southern Maine down to northern Florida and as far west as Michigan and Ohio. Within this range, these turtles make their homes in wetlands such as marshes, swamps, ponds, bogs, and slow-moving streams.

These turtles do well in environments with lots of aquatic plants and soft, muddy bottoms. The muddy areas give them places to burrow and hide from predators or rest during the colder months. Since spotted turtles are semi-aquatic, they spend time both in water and on land. They need land for basking in the sun, which helps them regulate their body temperature, and for nesting during the breeding season. Basking spots, like logs or rocks near water, are especially important for their health.

Spotted turtles are most active during the warmer months, especially in spring and early summer. During these times, you can often spot them sunning themselves on logs or rocks. When the weather gets too hot or cold, they may become less active, spending more time hiding in mud or underwater vegetation to stay cool or warm.

The spotted turtle's dependence on specific wetland habitats makes them vulnerable to environmental changes. Many of the wetlands they rely on are being destroyed or damaged by human activities. For example, urban development often involves draining or building over wetlands, leaving these turtles with fewer places to live. Pollution from farming, factories, and other sources can also harm their habitats, making the water unsafe for them. In addition, climate change can affect water levels and temperatures, further threatening their survival.

Because of these challenges, spotted turtle populations have declined in some areas. Conservation efforts are essential to protect these turtles and the habitats they need to survive. One important step is preserving and restoring wetlands, ensuring they remain safe and healthy environments for wildlife. Laws and regulations that prevent the destruction of wetlands or limit pollution can also help protect spotted turtles and other species that share their habitats.

People can also support spotted turtle conservation in smaller ways. Avoiding the collection of wild turtles is important because removing them from their natural habitats can hurt local populations. If you come across a spotted turtle in the wild, it is best to leave it where it is. Taking the time to learn about wetlands and why they are important can also encourage people to support conservation projects.

For those who enjoy seeing spotted turtles in nature, it's helpful to know that they are most often found in clean, undisturbed wetlands with plenty of plant life. Patience and quiet observation are key, as these turtles are shy and may hide if they feel threatened. By protecting their natural habitats and respecting their space, we can help ensure these beautiful turtles continue to thrive in the wild.

WHY CHOOSE SPOTTED TURTLES AS PETS?

Spotted turtles are a popular choice among reptile enthusiasts, and it's easy to see why. They are small, making them easier to care for compared to larger species of turtles. Their beautiful appearance, with bright yellow or orange spots on a dark shell, makes them visually striking and unique. On top of that, they have calm personalities, and their care needs are relatively simple, which makes them appealing as pets.

One of the main reasons people choose spotted turtles as pets is because of their interactive behavior. Unlike some reptiles that may be shy or hide away most of the time, spotted turtles are curious creatures. They are often seen approaching their owners, especially during feeding times. This curiosity and willingness to interact make them more engaging as pets. Unlike other reptiles that may keep to themselves, spotted turtles enjoy exploring their surroundings and can even seem to develop a bond with their owners. This interactive quality is one of the things that sets them apart from other reptiles.

Taking care of a spotted turtle involves creating a suitable environment that closely matches their natural habitat. They are semi-aquatic, so they need both water and land areas in their enclosure. The water section should be large enough for the turtle to swim and soak, and it should be kept clean and at the right temperature. The land area should have spots where the turtle can bask and warm up under a heat lamp, mimicking the sunbathing they would do in the wild. Additionally, providing the right lighting is important for their overall health, as it helps them regulate their internal clocks and supports their vitamin D production.

Their diet is another important factor in their care. Spotted turtles are omnivores, which means they eat both plants and small animals. A healthy diet for a spotted turtle includes a variety of foods such as insects, worms, leafy greens, and commercial turtle pellets. Feeding them a balanced diet ensures they stay healthy and active. It's essential to give them the right types of food and to avoid overfeeding, as this can lead to health issues.

When these basic needs are met, spotted turtles can thrive in captivity and live for many years, bringing joy to their owners. With the proper care, they can become a long-term companion, offering not just the joy of watching them explore but also the satisfaction of knowing you are providing a safe and healthy environment for them.

However, potential turtle owners should be aware that owning a spotted turtle is a big responsibility. One important consideration is the source of the turtle. It's crucial to ensure that any spotted turtle purchased as a pet has been ethically sourced. Wild turtles should not be taken from their natural habitats, as this can harm local populations and disrupt ecosystems. Ethically sourced turtles come from responsible breeders who raise them in captivity. By choosing these turtles, owners help protect wild populations and ensure the survival of the species.

Another factor to keep in mind is the long lifespan of spotted turtles. They can live for many decades, with some reaching 50 years or more. Owning a spotted turtle is a long-term commitment that requires planning and dedication. Potential owners should be prepared to care for the turtle for many years, ensuring that their needs are met throughout their life. This includes providing proper care as the turtle ages, making adjustments to their environment if necessary, and staying informed about their health and well-being.

Chapter 2

ACTIVITY PATTERNS AND SEASONAL CHANGES

Spotted turtles are cold-blooded, meaning their body temperature depends on the temperature of their environment. Because of this, their activity levels change with the seasons. In warmer months, especially during spring and summer, spotted turtles are much more active. They can often be seen basking in the sun, searching for food, or engaging in mating activities. However, when the weather gets colder, as in fall and winter, their activity slows down, and they enter a state called brumation. Brumation is similar to hibernation, but there are a few differences. While in brumation, the turtle's body functions slow down, and it becomes much less active. Occasionally, the turtle may wake up to drink some water or move a little, but it doesn't behave the way it does during the warmer months.

When the weather is warm, spotted turtles enjoy basking in the sun. They often do this on logs, rocks, or mud banks near the water. Basking is important for these turtles because it helps them regulate their body temperature, which is necessary since they can't generate heat on their own. It also allows them to make vitamin D, which is essential for absorbing calcium and keeping their shells and bones healthy. During the warmer months, spotted turtles are also more likely to forage for food. They eat a variety of things, including aquatic plants, insects, and small invertebrates. These are the foods that give them the nutrients they need to stay healthy and strong.

As the weather begins to cool down and the days get shorter, spotted turtles prepare for brumation. This is a period when their metabolism slows down, and they become less responsive to their surroundings. Instead of being active, they spend most of their time resting in the mud at the bottom of ponds or streams. This helps them stay warm because the mud provides insulation from the cold air above the water. While in brumation, spotted turtles do not eat, and their body processes slow significantly. It's a kind of rest that helps them conserve energy during the colder months when food is less abundant and temperatures are too low for them to be active.

Brumation is not the same as hibernation, although they are similar. While hibernating animals typically sleep through the winter, brumating animals like spotted turtles may wake up occasionally. They might drink water or move around a little, but they won't be actively foraging or hunting for food. Their energy use is much lower, and they simply rest and wait for the warmer months to return.

In general, the activity patterns of spotted turtles are closely tied to the seasons. During the warmer months, they are out and about, taking advantage of the heat to stay active, find food, and bask in the sun. As the temperature drops and the days become shorter, they slow down and enter brumation to survive the winter months. This cycle of activity and rest helps spotted turtles adapt to the changing environment, allowing them to stay healthy and safe in their natural habitats.

SOCIAL DYNAMICS: SOLITARY VS. GROUP LIVING

Spotted turtles are generally solitary animals. They prefer spending most of their time alone and are usually quite territorial, especially during the mating season. Unlike some other turtle species that live in large groups or herds, spotted turtles tend to avoid group living. However, there are certain times when they may be seen together in small groups, particularly when they are basking in the sun or when resources, such as food, are abundant.

In the wild, spotted turtles interact more with each other during the breeding season, which usually takes place in the spring. During this time, male turtles search for females. They often engage in courtship behaviors to attract the females. This can include chasing the female or gently nuzzling her shell. The male turtle may try to mount the female and, in some cases, perform a small ritual where he taps her face with his claws to signal his intentions. These courtship behaviors are part of their mating ritual, and the males are often quite persistent in their attempts to attract a mate.

Outside of the breeding season, spotted turtles usually live alone and are not very social. They are territorial animals and have specific areas they consider their home ranges. These ranges are places where they feel safe and secure, and they may defend them from other turtles. However, their territories are not always strictly defined, and sometimes the ranges of different turtles can overlap. When spotted turtles encounter each other, they usually do not engage in aggressive behavior. Instead, they will typically retreat or move away to avoid conflict.

Spotted turtles are peaceful by nature and do not often seek out interactions with other turtles, even if their home ranges overlap. If they do encounter another turtle, they usually avoid confrontation and may simply walk away. This is because spotted turtles are not as social as some other species, and they prefer to keep to themselves. They are not known for fighting or being aggressive, and they are more likely to peacefully coexist with other turtles as long as there is enough space and resources to go around.

When kept in captivity, spotted turtles can sometimes tolerate the presence of other turtles, but they still prefer to live alone. In an enclosure, it's important to provide enough space for each turtle so that they do not feel stressed or threatened. If there is not enough room, or if the turtles feel crowded, they may become territorial and start to show signs of dominance. For example, one turtle might push another away from a basking spot or food, trying to claim it as their own. These behaviors can be a sign of stress or competition, and they can be harmful to the turtles if not properly managed.

To avoid these problems, it's important to make sure that each turtle has plenty of space to roam and a place to bask or hide where they feel safe. Providing separate basking spots or feeding areas can help reduce territorial disputes. In some cases, it might be better to keep spotted turtles in separate enclosures to prevent any potential conflicts.

RECOGNIZING STRESS AND HEALTH ISSUES

Spotted turtles, like all reptiles, are sensitive to changes in their environment and can become stressed easily. When a turtle is stressed or unwell, it may show signs that something is wrong. These signs can include changes in behavior, appearance, and eating habits. For example, a stressed spotted turtle might spend more time basking, be hesitant to enter the water, lose its appetite, or have problems with its shell. It's important for turtle owners to watch for these signs so they can address any issues early on.

One of the most common causes of stress in spotted turtles is poor environmental conditions. Turtles need the right temperature, humidity, and light levels to stay healthy. If any of these factors are not ideal, the turtle can become stressed. For example, if the temperature is too cold, the turtle may spend too much time basking in an attempt to warm up. This can lead to lethargy, where the turtle is sluggish and doesn't move much. On the other hand, if the environment is too hot, the turtle might get stressed from the heat. This can lead to dehydration or difficulty regulating its body temperature, which is essential for its health.

Another cause of stress for spotted turtles is overcrowding. Spotted turtles are solitary creatures by nature, so they don't do well when kept with other turtles in a small space. If they don't have enough room to move around or their space is being invaded by another turtle, they can become anxious or aggressive. Competition for food and basking spots can also lead to stress. This is why it's important to give each turtle enough space and provide areas where they can hide or rest without being disturbed. A varied and balanced diet also helps to reduce stress and keep turtles healthy.

In addition to stress, health issues can also affect spotted turtles. One of the most common health problems is shell rot, which is usually caused by bacterial or fungal infections. Shell rot happens when the turtle's shell becomes soft, disfigured, or develops dark spots. This can occur if the turtle is kept in dirty water or if its shell is damaged. If a turtle has shell rot, it needs treatment as soon as possible to prevent further damage.

Respiratory infections are another common health issue. These infections can make it hard for a turtle to breathe properly and can cause symptoms such as wheezing, labored breathing, or discharge from the nose and eyes. Respiratory infections are often caused by cold or damp conditions. If the environment is too cold or humid, the turtle's respiratory system can become compromised. To prevent respiratory infections, it's essential to maintain the proper temperature and humidity levels in the turtle's habitat.

Parasites, such as internal worms, can also cause health problems for spotted turtles. These parasites can lead to weight loss, lethargy, and poor appetite. If a turtle is infected with parasites, it may become weak and stop eating. This is why it's important to check the turtle's health regularly and keep an eye out for any signs of illness.

The best way to catch health problems early is to observe the turtle closely. If you notice that the turtle is suddenly less active than usual, is not eating, or if there are changes in the appearance of its shell, these could be signs of a health problem. Any sudden or unusual behavior should be taken seriously. If you notice any of these signs, it's important to take the turtle to a veterinarian who specializes in reptiles. A vet will be able to examine the turtle, diagnose the problem, and recommend the right treatment to help the turtle recover.

Chapter 3

LAWS ON CAPTURING AND KEEPING SPOTTED TURTLES

T here are strict laws in place that control the capture and ownership of spotted turtles because they are protected in many areas of their native range. These laws are intended to prevent the over-exploitation of the species and help ensure their survival in the wild. In the United States, spotted turtles are considered a "species of concern" in many states, and some states have laws that make it illegal to capture, sell, or own them without the proper permits. If you're considering keeping a spotted turtle as a pet, it's very important to check the specific regulations in your state or region to avoid breaking any laws.

In states like Michigan, Ohio, and Indiana, the spotted turtle is a protected species, meaning it is illegal to capture them from the wild. In some other states, it may be legal to have a spotted turtle as a pet, but only if it was obtained from a licensed breeder or a pet store that follows legal and ethical guidelines. Some states even have specific rules about how many spotted turtles you can keep or whether you need a special permit to own one.

These laws are put in place to protect the species from over-collection. Spotted turtles are small and have a distinctive, striking appearance, which makes them desirable to pet owners. Unfortunately, this has led to illegal trapping and trafficking of spotted turtles, particularly for the pet trade. The demand for spotted turtles as pets has contributed to a decline in their population in the wild. Over-collecting wild turtles for sale or trade can harm the species and make it harder for the turtles to survive in their natural habitat.

Even if it may be legal to own a spotted turtle in certain areas, it's crucial to understand that removing them from the wild is often illegal and can harm the species in several ways. Wild-caught spotted turtles are not as likely to adapt to life in captivity. They might carry diseases or parasites that could harm other turtles or animals in captivity. Furthermore, taking turtles from their natural habitats can disrupt local ecosystems, affecting other plants and animals that rely on the same environment.

The act of taking turtles from the wild also poses a significant risk to the long-term survival of spotted turtles as a species. When turtles are removed from their natural habitat, they are no longer contributing to the reproduction of the species. This can lead to a decrease in the number of turtles in the wild, further threatening their population. Wild turtles play an important role in their ecosystems, and removing them disrupts the balance of nature. By following laws and ethical guidelines, we can help ensure that spotted turtles continue to thrive in the wild.

If you are interested in keeping a spotted turtle as a pet, it's essential to make sure that the turtle you obtain comes from a legal, ethical source, such as a licensed breeder or a pet store that follows the law. Captive-bred turtles are more likely to adjust to life in captivity and are not harming wild populations. Additionally, supporting ethical breeders and businesses that follow legal guidelines helps protect the species and ensure that the turtles you care for are healthy and well-treated.

CONSERVATION STATUS AND PROTECTION EFFORTS

Spotted turtles are classified as "vulnerable" on the International Union for Conservation of Nature (IUCN) Red List, which means that they are at risk of becoming endangered if current trends continue. Their populations have been decreasing because of several threats, such as habitat destruction, pollution, and the illegal pet trade. Wetland habitats, which are essential for spotted turtles, have been disappearing due to drainage or development for agriculture and urban expansion. This has reduced the turtles' access to the shallow, slow-moving waters they need for feeding, basking, and nesting.

The loss of these wetland habitats is a major factor in the decline of spotted turtle populations. Wetlands provide the right environment for turtles to find food, bask in the sun, and lay their eggs. When these areas are drained or turned into farmland or urban spaces, spotted turtles lose the places they need to survive. This is a significant challenge for the species, and it's crucial to protect and restore these habitats to help them recover.

To address these issues, many conservation efforts are underway to protect spotted turtles and their habitats. In some areas, organizations are working to restore wetlands by replanting vegetation, reducing pollution, and creating protected reserves where turtles can live safely, away from threats like habitat destruction. These efforts are important for preserving the ecosystems that spotted turtles depend on. Wetland restoration can also benefit other species that rely on the same habitat, helping to maintain biodiversity in the area.

In addition to habitat restoration, some states have enacted laws to help protect spotted turtles. These laws regulate or ban the capture and sale of spotted turtles to reduce illegal collection. The illegal pet trade is one of the main threats to spotted turtle populations, as turtles are often taken from the wild to be sold as pets. By making it illegal to capture or sell spotted turtles, these laws help ensure that the turtles stay in the wild where they belong.

Captive breeding programs are another important conservation tool. These programs aim to breed spotted turtles in controlled environments, such as zoos or breeding centers, and then release them back into their natural habitats. This helps boost the population of spotted turtles in the wild and reduces the pressure on wild populations caused by illegal collection. However, reintroducing turtles into the wild is a complex process. It requires careful planning to ensure that the released turtles have access to suitable habitats and can adapt to their natural environment. Reintroducing turtles also involves monitoring them to ensure that they are surviving and thriving in the wild.

Along with these efforts, individuals can play an important role in con-servation. Supporting organizations that work to protect turtles and their habitats is one way to help. People can also avoid buying wild-caught turtles, as this encourages illegal trapping and trade. It's important to follow legal regulations regarding the capture and ownership of turtles to ensure that they are not taken from the wild. By making responsible choices, people can contribute to the protection of spotted turtles and other wildlife.

ETHICAL GUIDELINES FOR RESPONSIBLE PET OWNERSHIP

If you're thinking about owning a spotted turtle, it's important to follow ethical guidelines to ensure the turtle's well-being and help protect the species. Responsible pet ownership goes beyond just following the law. It involves making sure the turtle is healthy, comfortable, and well taken care of for its entire life.

The first and most important guideline is to adopt, don't capture. Spotted turtles should not be taken from the wild. Wild turtles play a crucial role in their natural habitats, and capturing them harms both the turtles and the ecosystems they live in. If you want to own a spotted turtle, adopt one from a reputable breeder or rescue organization that follows ethical practices. Be cautious when buying from pet stores, as some may source their turtles from illegal or harmful suppliers. Always make sure the turtle you acquire comes from a responsible and sustainable source.

Spotted turtles also need a proper habitat to live in. This means providing both land and water areas. The water should be shallow, clean, and free from harmful chemicals. It's important to make sure that the water temperature is kept within the correct range and that the water quality is high. The land area should have hiding spots and basking areas, as these turtles like to hide and enjoy the warmth of the sun. The enclosure should be spacious enough for the turtle to move around and explore, as they are naturally curious. In addition to having a good space, the temperature and humidity levels must be carefully controlled. Spotted turtles need access to UVB light, which helps them absorb calcium and stay healthy. Providing the right environment is essential for their overall health and happiness.

When it comes to diet and nutrition, spotted turtles are omnivores, which means they eat both plants and animals. Their diet should consist of a variety of food sources, including aquatic plants, insects, small invertebrates, and sometimes fish. It's important to give them a balanced diet that mimics what they would eat in the wild. This diet should provide the necessary vitamins and minerals to keep their bones and shell strong. A poor diet can lead to health problems, so it's essential to provide proper nutrition for the turtle's growth and well-being.

Another important aspect of responsible ownership is avoiding overcrowding. Spotted turtles are solitary animals by nature. They do not do well living with other turtles unless there is plenty of space and the conditions are perfect. If multiple turtles are kept together in too small of an area, they can become stressed and may fight over food or basking spots. Overcrowding can lead to aggression, territorial disputes, and health problems for the turtles. Each turtle should have enough space to roam freely and access the resources it needs without competition or stress.

In addition to providing a good environment and diet, it's also important to give your turtle regular veterinary care. Just like any pet, spotted turtles need regular check-ups to stay healthy. Finding a veterinarian who has experience with reptiles is very important because they will understand the specific needs of a turtle. Regular visits can help catch any potential health problems early, such as shell rot, respiratory infections, or parasites. A vet can also provide advice on proper care and treatment if health issues arise.

Chapter 4

SIGNS OF A HEALTHY TURTLE

When selecting a spotted turtle, it's important to look for signs that indicate the turtle is healthy. A healthy turtle will show certain physical traits and behaviors that you can easily observe. These signs are key to ensuring you are bringing home a turtle that is in good condition and ready to thrive in its new environment.

First, check the turtle's eyes and nose. The eyes of a healthy spotted turtle should be clear and bright, with no cloudiness or discharge. If the eyes appear swollen or dull, or if there is any mucus or discharge coming from the nose, this could be a sign of a respiratory infection. Respiratory problems are common in turtles and can indicate poor living conditions, so it's important to avoid turtles with these symptoms.

Next, observe the turtle's behavior. A healthy spotted turtle should be active and alert. It should move around its environment, bask regularly, and engage in natural behaviors such as foraging or exploring its space. Turtles that are lethargic or seem unresponsive may be ill or stressed. Healthy turtles are curious and show interest in their surroundings, so if the turtle appears slow to react or seems overly tired, this could be a sign that something is wrong.

Another important thing to check is the turtle's shell. The shell of a healthy spotted turtle should be hard and smooth, with no cracks, soft spots, or visible scars. A smooth, intact shell is a sign that the turtle has been well cared for and is healthy. If the shell has any soft areas or signs of damage, it may indicate a problem, such as shell rot. Shell rot is a bacterial or fungal infection that can cause the shell to soften and become discolored. Be sure to inspect the shell carefully for any irregularities or signs of illness.

You should also pay attention to the turtle's breathing. Healthy turtles breathe easily and quietly. There should be no wheezing, labored breathing, or gurgling sounds. If a turtle is having difficulty breathing, it may be suffering from a respiratory infection or other health issues. You should listen closely for any abnormal sounds when the turtle breathes. If you notice any signs of distress while breathing, it is best to avoid purchasing the turtle, as respiratory problems can be serious and may require immediate veterinary attention.

The skin of a healthy spotted turtle should also be smooth and free from any lesions, sores, or swelling. It is normal for turtles to shed some skin, but large patches of skin shedding or abnormal growths can indicate a problem, such as a fungal or bacterial infection. Check the skin, especially around the limbs, neck, and under the shell, for any signs of unusual marks or bumps. If the skin looks irritated or damaged, this could be a sign of an infection that needs to be addressed.

Finally, observe the turtle's appetite. A healthy spotted turtle will have a good appetite and will eat regularly. If the turtle refuses food for an extended period, this could be a sign of stress, illness, or an inadequate diet. Healthy turtles are typically eager to eat and show interest in their food. If the turtle is not eating or is slow to take food, it's important to consider the possibility of health problems. A consistent and healthy appetite is a good indicator that the turtle is in good condition.

AVOIDING COMMON HEALTH ISSUES IN NEWLY ACQUIRED TURTLES

When you bring home a new turtle, it's important to be aware that they can sometimes develop health issues due to stress, changes in their environment, or problems that may not be immediately noticeable. Even if you selected a healthy turtle, there are some common health problems that you should watch for and try to prevent. Here are the most common health issues in newly acquired turtles and tips for avoiding them:

One of the most common health problems in turtles is respiratory infections. These infections are often caused by cold, damp environments or poor ventilation. Symptoms can include wheezing, labored breathing, nasal discharge, or swelling around the eyes and neck. To prevent respiratory infections, it's important to make sure your turtle's living space is warm, dry, and well-ventilated. Make sure you provide proper heating and UVB lighting, as these are essential for the turtle's immune system and overall health. Turtles need a warm environment to stay healthy, so maintaining a temperature that suits them is crucial to preventing respiratory issues.

Another health issue to be aware of is shell rot, which is a bacterial or fungal infection that can affect a turtle's shell. It usually starts with softening or discoloration of the shell, and if not treated, it can lead to more serious damage. Shell rot can be caused by a dirty or wet environment. To avoid this issue, it's essential to keep the turtle's habitat clean and dry. Make sure the water in the tank is changed regularly, and avoid keeping the turtle in stagnant water. Regularly clean the tank and ensure that the water is free from harmful bacteria that can cause infection.

Parasites are another common problem that turtles can face. These can be internal parasites like worms or protozoa, or external parasites like mites. Symptoms of a parasite problem may include weight loss, lack of appetite, abnormal droppings, or excessive scratching. To prevent parasites, it's important to ensure that your turtle comes from a clean environment. If you are introducing a new turtle to your home, it's a good idea to quarantine it for a few weeks before placing it in the same tank as any other turtles you may already have. This will help to ensure that the new turtle does not introduce any parasites into the existing habitat. A clean living space is essential for keeping parasites at bay.

Dehydration is another concern, especially because spotted turtles are semi-aquatic and need access to water at all times. If a turtle becomes dehydrated, it can show signs like lethargy, loss of appetite, and sunken eyes. To prevent dehydration, make sure your turtle always has access to clean, fresh water for drinking and swimming. The water should be at the right temperature, and it's important to change the water regularly to avoid harmful bacteria from growing. Dehydration can weaken a turtle's health, so it's essential to ensure the turtle's water needs are met consistently.

Stress is another major factor in a turtle's health. Stress can weaken the turtle's immune system, making it more vulnerable to illness. Stress is often caused by overcrowding, sudden changes in the environment, or poor living conditions. For example, if the turtle's habitat is too small or not properly set up, it can cause stress. To minimize stress, make sure your turtle's environment is as stable and comfortable as possible. The habitat should mimic the turtle's natural environment, with both land and water areas, proper lighting, and temperature. Try to keep the environment quiet and calm to reduce any external stressors.

CHOOSING REPUTABLE BREEDERS OR RESCUE ORGANIZATIONS

When you decide to get a spotted turtle, it is important to choose a trustworthy breeder or rescue organization. This ensures that the turtle is ethically sourced and raised in healthy conditions. Here are some key points to consider when selecting a reputable breeder or rescue group:

First, do your research. Look for breeders or rescue organizations that have a good reputation and a history of ethical practices. Check online reviews and ask other turtle owners for recommendations. Reputable breeders and rescue organizations will be transparent about their practices, including how they breed, care for, and house their turtles. They should also be willing to answer your questions and provide you with useful information about their operations. Researching is crucial because it helps you avoid organizations that may not care for their turtles properly or may not follow ethical guidelines.

Second, always ask about the turtle's history. A responsible breeder or rescue organization should be able to provide information about the turtle's background. This includes details about its age, health status, and whether it has had any previous medical treatment. They should also be able to discuss the turtle's behavior, diet, and how it has been cared for. This helps you understand the turtle's needs and any specific care it might require. Knowing the turtle's history allows you to ensure that the animal is healthy and that there are no hidden issues that could affect its well-being in the future.

Third, make sure the breeder or rescue organization provides proper care and housing. Before you decide to purchase or adopt a turtle, visit the facility and check the living conditions. The turtle's enclosure should be clean, spacious, and well-maintained. It should include areas for both land and water, as these turtles need both environments to thrive. The turtles should be housed in conditions that allow them to behave naturally, with access to basking spots and clean water for swimming. Ensuring that the turtles live in a suitable habitat is a sign that the breeder or rescue group is dedicated to the health and well-being of the animals.

Fourth, always avoid wild-caught turtles. Wild-caught turtles often face higher risks of disease, stress, and difficulty adapting to life in captivity. It is best to choose turtles that have been bred in captivity. These turtles are generally healthier and more accustomed to life in a home environment. Wild-caught turtles can also carry diseases or parasites that could be harmful to other turtles or pets in your home. By choosing a captive-bred turtle, you are helping to reduce the demand for wild-caught turtles and supporting ethical breeding practices.

Fifth, ask for a health guarantee. A reputable breeder or rescue organization should offer a health guarantee or at least have a clear return policy. This means that if the turtle shows signs of illness shortly after you bring it home, you can take steps to address the problem. A health guarantee ensures that you are getting a healthy turtle and gives you peace of mind. It also shows that the breeder or rescue organization stands behind the quality of the animals they provide.

Chapter 5

INDOOR ENCLOSURE SETUP

If you want to keep a spotted turtle indoors, it's important to create an environment that allows the turtle to behave naturally. A good indoor enclosure will give your turtle access to water, a basking area, and plenty of space to move around and explore.

First, the size of the enclosure is crucial. Even though spotted turtles are small, they still need room to move. For a single turtle, the minimum size of the enclosure should be a 40-gallon tank, but larger tanks are always better. A tank that is at least 36 inches long will give the turtle enough space to swim, bask, and explore. If you plan to keep more than one turtle, the enclosure will need to be larger to prevent crowding.

Next, the water area is an essential part of the enclosure because spotted turtles are semi-aquatic animals. They need access to clean water to swim and stay hydrated. The water should cover at least half of the floor space of the tank, and it should be deep enough for the turtle to swim comfortably. A water depth of about 4-6 inches is perfect, but the water should be deep enough for the turtle to fully submerge. It is very important to keep the water clean to avoid bacteria or waste buildup, so a good filtration system is highly recommended. This will help keep the water fresh and safe for your turtle.

A basking area is also necessary for spotted turtles. These turtles need a warm, dry area to bask in because they rely on sunlight, or UVB light, to regulate their body temperature and absorb vitamins like vitamin D3. In an indoor enclosure, you can create a basking platform using a flat rock, a piece of wood, or a floating dock. The basking area should be placed under a heat lamp to maintain a temperature of 85-90°F (29-32°C). It is important to create a temperature gradient by positioning the heat source at one end of the tank. This will allow your turtle to move between warmer and cooler areas of the tank, helping it regulate its body temperature.

Lighting is another important aspect of the enclosure. Spotted turtles need UVB light to produce vitamin D3, which is necessary for absorbing calcium and keeping their shells healthy. The UVB light should be placed above the basking area so the turtle can get the necessary exposure. UVB bulbs lose their effectiveness over time, so it's important to replace them every 6 to 12 months. To ensure that your turtle gets a proper day and night cycle, you can use a timer to regulate the lighting and provide a dark period each night. This helps mimic the natural light cycle and keeps the turtle's environment healthy.

Temperature and humidity are also key factors in maintaining a healthy enclosure. The temperature in the cooler areas of the tank should be around 75°F (24°C), while the warmer basking areas should stay between 85-90°F (29-32°C). This range of temperatures allows the turtle to regulate its body heat. The humidity level is just as important, as it helps with shedding and keeps the turtle healthy. A humidity level of 60-70% is ideal for spotted turtles. You can maintain the right humidity by misting the enclosure regularly and providing a water dish large enough for the turtle to soak in. This will help ensure that the environment remains comfortable for the turtle.

OUTDOOR PONDS: DESIGN AND MAINTENANCE

If you have enough space and live in a suitable climate, an outdoor pond can be a wonderful way to keep a spotted turtle. It provides a more natural environment where the turtle can enjoy sunlight, swim, bask, and explore in a larger area.

When designing your pond, it should have both shallow and deep areas. Shallow areas are essential for the turtle to bask in the sun and nest. Deeper areas, with a depth of about 12-18 inches, are necessary for swimming and for the turtle to escape from potential predators. The edges of the pond should be gently sloping to make it easy for the turtle to enter and exit the water. It's also important that the pond is well-drained to prevent stagnant water, which can lead to the growth of harmful bacteria that may affect the turtle's health.

Maintaining clean water is very important for the well-being of your spotted turtle. You should use a good filtration system that is suitable for the size of your pond. Regularly check the water's pH, temperature, and clarity to ensure it is safe for the turtle. Cleaning the pond as needed is also important. If your pond is large, you may not need to change the water often, but during warmer months, when algae and debris can build up quickly, it's a good idea to change the water every few weeks to keep it fresh.

Outdoor ponds should have basking areas where the turtle can sit and enjoy the sun. You can create these areas using natural materials like logs, rocks, or raised platforms. These basking spots should be stable and placed in sunny areas, as the turtle needs sunlight to regulate its body temperature and get UVB rays, which are important for its health. It's also a good idea to have both sunny and shaded spots in the pond. This way, the turtle can move between warm and cooler areas to help maintain its body temperature naturally.

Spotted turtles need places to hide and feel safe. You can add dense plants along the pond's edges or submerged rocks and driftwood to provide these hiding spots. Adding a small shelter, like a partially submerged log, will also give the turtle a place to seek refuge if it feels threatened. If you live in an area with predators such as birds of prey, raccoons, or domestic pets, it's important to provide extra protection for your turtle. You could install a secure mesh fence or cover the pond with an enclosure to prevent predators from reaching the turtle.

In colder climates, where the temperature drops in winter, spotted turtles may go into a state called brumation, which is similar to hibernation. During brumation, the turtle becomes inactive and its metabolism slows down. If your pond is in an area that freezes during the winter, you'll need to take special care. If the pond is deep enough, the turtle can survive the winter by staying in the deeper parts of the pond, where the water temperature remains above freezing. However, if your pond freezes completely, you may need to bring the turtle inside and set up an indoor enclosure to keep it safe during the cold months.

OPTIMAL SUBSTRATE AND DECORATIONS

When setting up an enclosure for your spotted turtle, whether indoors or outdoors, it's important to choose the right substrate and decorations. These elements not only help create a comfortable and safe environment for your turtle but also make the space more natural and visually appealing.

For indoor enclosures, you'll need to use different types of substrate for the water and land areas. In the water section, smooth river rocks or gravel are ideal. The rocks should be large enough so that the turtle cannot swallow them, as small rocks could lead to choking or intestinal blockages. The water area should be designed so that the turtle can swim and move around without the risk of ingesting any harmful objects.

In the land area, it's a good idea to use a mix of coconut coir, soil, and sand. This natural substrate gives the turtle a soft surface to walk on and provides the opportunity to dig. Spotted turtles enjoy digging, and this substrate allows them to engage in this natural behavior. It also helps to keep the environment clean and dry. However, you should avoid using fine sand or gravel in the land area, as the turtle may accidentally ingest it, which could lead to health problems.

For outdoor ponds, the substrate should be simple and natural. Clean, non-toxic rocks and pebbles are great options for both appearance and functionality. These rocks provide a natural look to the pond and are easy to clean. If you want to add some plants to your outdoor pond, you can include aquatic plants like water lilies or submerged plants. These plants provide additional shelter and hiding spots for your turtle. They also help to maintain the quality of the water by absorbing excess nutrients, which can help prevent algae growth and keep the pond clean.

When decorating your turtle's enclosure, it's important to think about both the turtle's safety and its natural behaviors. Decorations like rocks, driftwood, and plants can make the enclosure more interesting and enjoyable for the turtle. These items provide hiding spots where the turtle can feel secure, as well as areas for basking. Having a variety of these items also gives the turtle places to explore, mimicking the natural environment they would experience in the wild.

In addition to making the enclosure visually appealing, the decorations also help the turtle in other ways. For instance, live plants can provide food and shelter for the turtle. Aquatic plants like duckweed, anacharis, or water hyacinth are beneficial for the turtle's diet, as they may occasionally nibble on them. Plants also help improve the water quality by absorbing excess nutrients that could otherwise lead to water pollution.

When choosing plants for your turtle's enclosure, it's important to make sure they are safe and non-toxic. Some plants may be harmful to turtles if they nibble on them, so it's a good idea to do research before introducing any new plants. You can also choose plants that are native to the turtle's natural habitat, as this helps create a more authentic environment.

Both indoor and outdoor enclosures benefit from the right substrates and decorations. In indoor setups, smooth rocks in the water and a mix of coconut coir, soil, and sand in the land area provide the turtle with a comfortable, safe, and natural environment. In outdoor ponds, clean rocks and aquatic plants add beauty to the pond while also offering shelter and maintaining water quality. Decorations like rocks, driftwood, and plants offer places for the turtle to hide, bask, and explore, all of which contribute to its well-being.

Chapter 6

IDEAL TEMPERATURE AND LIGHTING CONDITIONS

S potted turtles, like all reptiles, are ectothermic, which means they depend on external sources of heat to regulate their body temperature. In the wild, they bask in the sun to warm up and retreat to cooler spots when they need to lower their body temperature. To keep your spotted turtle healthy in captivity, you need to provide the right temperature and lighting conditions, both in indoor enclosures and outdoor ponds.

Temperature Requirements

Basking Area: The basking area is where your spotted turtle will go to warm up. This area should be kept at a temperature between 85-90°F (29-32°C). This range is ideal for your turtle to regulate its body temperature. If the basking area is too cool, the turtle may become sluggish, and its immune system might weaken, making it more prone to illnesses. If the temperature is too high, the turtle could experience heat stress, which can be harmful to its health.

Water Temperature: The water in the enclosure is another important factor in maintaining the turtle's health. The water should be kept between 70-75°F (21-24°C) for optimal health. Water that is too cold can cause the turtle to become inactive and sluggish, while water that is too warm can cause stress and health problems, such as respiratory issues. It is important to monitor the water temperature carefully to ensure the turtle's comfort.

Ambient Temperature: The ambient temperature refers to the temperature in the cooler areas of the enclosure. This should be maintained around 75°F (24°C). Having a cooler side in the enclosure, along with the warmer basking area, creates a temperature gradient. This allows the turtle to move between warmer and cooler zones depending on what it needs to regulate its body temperature.

Heating the Enclosure

If your spotted turtle is housed indoors, you will need to provide a heat source to maintain the proper temperatures. Use a heat lamp or a ceramic heater placed above the basking area to achieve the correct temperature. It's important to position the heat lamp at a safe distance to avoid overheating your turtle. The heat source should create a warm basking spot, but it should not make the whole enclosure too hot. You can also use an aquarium heater to help regulate the water temperature, especially if the turtle is in a tank or large aquarium.

Lighting Needs

In addition to heating, spotted turtles require proper lighting to stay healthy. UVB and UVA light are essential for their well-being. UVB light helps turtles produce vitamin D3, which is important for absorbing calcium and maintaining a strong, healthy shell. UVA light, on the other hand, helps regulate natural behaviors, such as feeding, mating, and overall activity.

UVB Lighting: A UVB bulb should be installed in the enclosure to simulate sunlight. The UVB light should be positioned directly over the basking area so the turtle can absorb the rays while basking. These UVB bulbs should be replaced every 6 to 12 months, as their effectiveness decreases over time. It is important to use a bulb specifically designed for reptiles, as regular light bulbs do not provide the necessary UVB rays that turtles need for their health.

UVA Lighting: UVA light also plays a key role in a turtle's health. While UVB is necessary for the turtle's shell and calcium absorption, UVA lighting helps regulate the turtle's daily cycle and supports natural behaviors. Using a combined UVA/UVB bulb is a great way to meet both lighting needs in one fixture.

Light Cycle: It is important to follow a natural light cycle for your turtle. Both UVB and UVA lights should be turned on for 10-12 hours during the day to simulate the natural sun cycle. At night, the lights should be turned off to create a dark period, which helps your turtle maintain a healthy sleep-wake cycle.

PROVIDING A BASKING AREA

A basking area is very important for spotted turtles to help them regulate their body temperature, dry off, and absorb UVB light. In their natural habitat, spotted turtles often bask on logs, rocks, or other raised surfaces near the water. To provide a suitable basking area in captivity, you need to pay attention to the size, materials, and positioning of the basking spot.

Creating the Basking Area:

Platform: The basking platform should be sturdy and large enough for the turtle to fully stretch out and bask comfortably. It should be made of materials like flat rocks, a floating dock, or a piece of wood. The surface must not be too steep or slippery, as the turtle needs to be able to climb up onto the platform with ease. If the platform is difficult to climb, the turtle may not use it, which could lead to health problems.

Positioning: The basking area should be placed in a spot where it will receive plenty of heat from a heat lamp and UVB light. The ideal location is directly under the light source so the turtle can warm up efficiently. This ensures that the turtle gets enough heat and UVB rays to regulate its body temperature and absorb essential vitamins. If your turtle is kept outdoors, place the basking area in a sunny spot where it can get natural sunlight. However, if the outdoor temperature is too high, make sure the turtle has access to shaded areas to cool down.

Dry Surface: It is important that the basking area stays dry and is elevated above the water level. When the turtle basks, it needs to be dry to avoid the risk of shell rot and other health problems. If the turtle spends too much time wet while basking, it can cause damage to its shell and skin, leading to infections or other issues. Therefore, the platform should be high enough that the turtle can stay completely dry while basking. Ensure that the area is not in the water or surrounded by dampness, as this can make the turtle prone to health problems like shell rot.

Basking Time: Spotted turtles need regular access to basking areas to stay healthy. Basking helps them regulate their body temperature, dry off after swimming, and get the UVB light they need for calcium absorption. In the wild, spotted turtles bask for several hours each day, especially during warmer months, and they rely on the sun to help them stay warm and healthy. In captivity, providing a reliable and consistent basking area ensures that the turtle can meet its natural needs.

It is important to allow the turtle to bask for several hours each day. This regular basking time helps the turtle stay active and supports its overall health. Without a proper basking area, a turtle may not be able to maintain a healthy body temperature or absorb enough vitamin D3, which can lead to weakened bones, shell deformities, and other health issues.

WATER QUALITY AND FILTRATION SYSTEMS

Water quality is extremely important for the health of spotted turtles, as they spend a lot of time in the water. Dirty water can lead to serious health problems like infections, parasites, and shell rot. To keep your turtle healthy, it is essential to maintain clean water. This can be done by using a proper filtration system, regularly changing the water, and monitoring the water conditions.

Water Filtration: A good filtration system is necessary to keep the water clean and free of harmful waste products. The filter should be strong enough to handle the size of your turtle's tank or pond and keep the water constantly circulating. In smaller tanks or enclosures, a canister filter or submersible filter works well because it can manage the waste load and keep the water clean. For outdoor ponds, you may need a larger, external filter to ensure the water stays clear and healthy for your turtle.

Water Quality Parameters: To keep your turtle safe and healthy, it's important to check and maintain several water quality parameters. These include the pH level, ammonia, nitrites, nitrates, and water temperature.

· pH Level: The water should have a neutral to slightly alkaline pH, ideally around 7.0 to 7.5. You can test the water using a pH test kit to make sure it stays within this range. If the pH level is too low or too high, it can cause stress for the turtle and lead to health issues. Regular testing helps ensure that the pH level remains stable.

• Ammonia, Nitrites, and Nitrates: These are harmful compounds that can build up in the water from waste, leftover food, and decaying plant matter. Ammonia and nitrites are especially toxic to turtles. It's important to regularly test for these compounds and keep their levels as low as possible. Doing regular water changes and using an effective filter helps keep ammonia, nitrites, and nitrates under control.

• Water Temperature: Spotted turtles need water that is kept at the right temperature. The ideal range for water temperature is between 70–75°F (21–24°C). If the water is too cold, the turtle may become sluggish, while water that is too warm can cause stress. Use a thermometer to keep track of the water temperature and make adjustments if needed to maintain the right temperature.

Water Changes: Even with a good filtration system, you still need to change the water regularly to keep it clean. As a general guideline, change 20–30% of the water every week. This may vary depending on the size of the tank or pond, the number of turtles you have, and how well the filtration system works. If your turtle lives in a larger outdoor pond, water changes may be needed less often, but you should still monitor the water quality to ensure it remains clean.

In an outdoor pond, you may also want to consider adding plants that help filter the water naturally. Aquatic plants can absorb excess nutrients, which helps prevent the growth of algae and keeps the water cleaner. However, even with plants, you should still use a good filtration system and regularly check the water quality.

Chapter 7

NATURAL DIET IN THE WILD

I n the wild, spotted turtles are opportunistic feeders, meaning they eat a variety of foods depending on what is available to them. Their diet includes plants, small invertebrates, and some aquatic animals. Understanding what they eat in the wild helps us provide them with the right nutrition when they are kept in captivity.

Spotted turtles eat a variety of plant matter. They feed on different types of aquatic plants, such as algae, aquatic weeds, and water lilies. These plants are an important part of their diet because they provide vitamins, minerals, and fiber, which helps with digestion. Spotted turtles also eat fruits and berries that fall into the water, as well as seeds and other vegetation that grow around wetland areas. These plants offer the turtle important nutrients needed for their health.

In addition to plants, spotted turtles also eat small invertebrates, which are animals without backbones, such as insects, worms, snails, and crustaceans. During the spring and summer months, when food is plentiful, spotted turtles actively search for these protein-rich foods. Protein is essential for their growth, shell development, and overall health. It helps them build strong shells and maintain their energy levels.

While not a major part of their diet, spotted turtles may also eat small fish or amphibians when they have the opportunity. This includes tadpoles, young frogs, and other small aquatic animals. These animal proteins are a good source of nutrition, especially when they are easy to find. In the wild, these foods supplement the turtle's regular diet, helping to provide additional protein and nutrients.

Overall, the natural diet of a spotted turtle is balanced, with about 70% plant matter and 30% animal protein. However, this balance can change depending on factors such as the turtle's age, the season, and the availability of food in their environment. For example, during certain times of the year when plant food is abundant, the turtle may eat more plants, while during other times, they may consume more animal protein.

In their natural environment, spotted turtles have access to a wide range of food sources that vary throughout the year. This diet helps them stay healthy and active. When kept in captivity, it is important to try to replicate this natural diet to ensure that the turtle gets all the nutrients it needs. By providing a mix of plant matter and animal protein, turtle owners can help their spotted turtles thrive and remain healthy.

Understanding what spotted turtles eat in the wild gives us a better idea of what to feed them in captivity. Their diet should include a variety of plants, such as aquatic plants, fruits, and seeds, as well as small invertebrates like insects and worms. Offering a mix of these foods will help ensure that the turtle receives the proper nutrition and stays healthy. Additionally, occasional animal proteins like small fish or amphibians can be included to supplement the diet, just as they would in the wild.

PREPARING A BALANCED DIET FOR CAPTIVE TURTLES

Providing a balanced diet for a captive spotted turtle is essential for maintaining its health. A diet similar to what it would eat in the wild helps prevent nutrient deficiencies and supports its growth, shell health, and overall activity.

In captivity, commercial turtle food like pellets and freeze-dried insects can be convenient, but it should not be the main food source. High-quality commercial food can supplement a more natural diet but should only make up a small part of the turtle's meals.

The majority of a spotted turtle's diet should be fresh vegetables and greens.

These vegetables provide important vitamins, minerals, and fiber, which are crucial for digestion and overall health. Some good options for leafy greens include collard greens, dandelion greens, and mustard greens. These greens are rich in nutrients and mimic the types of plants turtles would find in their natural habitat. Aquatic plants such as water lettuce, water hyacinth, and duckweed are also great choices since they closely resemble what turtles eat in the wild. In addition to leafy greens and aquatic plants, you can offer other vegetables like bell peppers, shredded carrots, and squash. These vegetables add variety and provide additional nutrients for your turtle.

Protein is another essential part of a spotted turtle's diet, especially for younger turtles or during the feeding season. You can provide various animal-based foods to give the protein your turtle needs. Insects like crickets, mealworms, and waxworms are good protein sources. You can also offer aquatic invertebrates such as snails, shrimp, and earthworms. These types of foods are similar to what turtles eat in the wild, helping to support their growth and overall health. Occasionally, you can offer small pieces of fresh fish, but fish should not be the main protein source. Hard-boiled eggs can also be fed in moderation as a protein supplement, but they should not be given too often.

Fruits can be offered to your spotted turtle as an occasional treat, but they should not make up a large part of the diet because they are high in sugar. Suitable fruits for spotted turtles include berries like strawberries, blueberries, and raspberries, as well as apples (without seeds) and pears. Melons, such as watermelon or cantaloupe, are also good options. These fruits can provide extra vitamins and moisture, but it's important to remember that they should be fed sparingly.

Calcium and Vitamin D3 are crucial for a turtle's health, especially for maintaining strong shells and bones. In the wild, spotted turtles get calcium from the plants they eat and from small aquatic animals that contain calcium in their shells or exoskeletons. In captivity, you can provide calcium supplements by sprinkling calcium powder on their food. Vitamin D3 is necessary for calcium absorption, and UVB lighting is essential for turtles to produce this vitamin. Be sure to provide the right lighting to help your turtle absorb calcium and maintain a healthy shell.

When feeding insects to your spotted turtle, it's a good idea to "gut-load" them before offering them as food. This means feeding the insects nutritious food like vegetables or calcium-rich supplements for 24-48 hours before feeding them to the turtle. This ensures the insects are rich in nutrients like calcium, fiber, and vitamins, which will then be passed on to your turtle when it eats the insect.

SAFE AND UNSAFE FOODS

When feeding spotted turtles, it's important to know which foods are safe and which ones could cause health problems. Not all foods are suitable for these turtles, and feeding them the wrong foods can lead to illnesses or even be life-threatening. Understanding safe and unsafe foods will help you provide a healthy diet for your spotted turtle.

Safe foods for spotted turtles include a variety of leafy greens, vegetables, fruits, invertebrates, and aquatic plants. Leafy greens like collard greens, dandelion greens, mustard greens, and kale are all excellent choices. These greens are rich in vitamins and minerals, helping to keep your turtle healthy. Vegetables such as squash, carrots (in small amounts), bell peppers, and peas are also good additions to your turtle's diet. These vegetables provide essential nutrients and fiber, supporting the turtle's digestion and overall well-being.

Invertebrates like crickets, worms, snails, and shrimp are great protein sources for your turtle. These small creatures are rich in protein and help support your turtle's growth and shell health. Fruits such as apples (without seeds), strawberries, blueberries, and melon can also be given as treats, but they should be fed in moderation. These fruits provide extra vitamins and hydration but should not make up a large part of the diet due to their high sugar content.

Aquatic plants such as water lettuce, water hyacinth, and duckweed are also safe and natural foods for spotted turtles. These plants not only provide food but also replicate the turtle's natural environment. You can also offer protein sources such as fish (in small amounts), eggs (in moderation), and earthworms, which help provide the necessary nutrients for a healthy shell and strong bones.

However, there are some foods that are unsafe for spotted turtles and should be avoided. Iceberg lettuce is one food to stay away from. While small amounts won't cause harm, it has very little nutritional value and can lead to diarrhea in turtles. It's best to avoid it altogether. Processed or salty foods like bread, deli meats, or anything with added salt or preservatives should never be given to your turtle. These foods can upset their digestive system and cause long-term health issues.

Citrus fruits such as oranges, lemons, and limes should also be avoided because of their high acidity. The acidity can cause digestive problems and discomfort for the turtle. Tomato leaves or stems should also be kept away from your turtle. While the fruit itself is safe in small quantities, the leaves and stems contain solanine, a toxin that can be harmful or even deadly to turtles if ingested.

Onions, garlic, and chives are also toxic to many animals, including turtles. These foods can cause serious health problems, so it is important never to feed them to your turtle. Any food that is not part of the natural diet, especially those that are spicy, overly salty, or contain preservatives, can be dangerous.

To ensure a healthy diet for your spotted turtle, it's important to provide a balanced mix of both plant and animal-based foods. A good general rule is that about 70% of the turtle's diet should consist of plant matter, and 30% should come from animal protein. However, this ratio can change depending on the turtle's age and activity level. Young turtles may require more protein for growth, while older turtles may need more plant matter.

Chapter 8

IDENTIFYING MALES AND FEMALES

To successfully breed spotted turtles, it is important to be able to tell the difference between males and females. While male and female spotted turtles may look alike at first glance, there are key physical and behavioral traits that can help you identify their gender. Learning to recognize these differences will help ensure proper care and successful breeding.

One of the easiest ways to distinguish between male and female spotted turtles is by examining the underside of their shells, called the plastron. Male spotted turtles have a concave plastron, meaning it curves inward slightly. This shape helps them mount the female during mating. On the other hand, females have a flat or slightly convex plastron. This design gives them extra space for carrying eggs inside their bodies, an essential adaptation for reproduction.

Another physical difference lies in the size and shape of their tails. Males have longer and thicker tails compared to females. Additionally, the cloacal opening, which is the vent used for reproduction and waste elimination, is positioned farther from the base of the tail in males. In females, the tail is shorter and thinner, and their cloacal opening is located closer to the base of the tail. This difference in tail size and placement is one of the clearest ways to identify the gender of your turtle.

The size of the turtle's body can also give you clues. Female spotted turtles are generally larger than males when they are fully grown. This size difference is particularly noticeable in adult turtles and serves an important purpose: larger females are better able to carry and lay eggs. In contrast, males are slightly smaller and more slender in build.

The shape of the shell, or carapace, is another feature to observe. Males often have a more elongated shell, while females tend to have a rounder and wider shell. While this difference can be subtle, it becomes easier to notice as the turtles grow older.

In addition to physical traits, behavioral differences can also help you determine the gender of your spotted turtles. Males are typically more active and may exhibit aggressive behavior, especially during the breeding season. During this time, males may chase after females and show courtship behaviors, such as nudging or biting the female's shell. These behaviors are part of the male's attempt to attract the female and initiate mating.

Females, on the other hand, are generally calmer and less active than males. They do not display the same aggressive or courting behaviors. Instead, they focus on finding suitable areas for laying their eggs after mating. Observing these behaviors over time can provide additional confirmation of the turtle's gender.

It is important to note that some of these differences may not be immediately visible in young turtles. Juveniles often look very similar regardless of gender, and these characteristics become more noticeable as the turtles mature. Most spotted turtles reach sexual maturity between the ages of 7 and 10 years. At this point, the physical and behavioral differences between males and females become clearer.

To accurately identify the gender of your spotted turtles, it is helpful to observe several traits rather than relying on just one. For example, examining the plastron, tail size, and cloacal opening together can give you a more reliable determination. Watching their behavior, especially during the breeding season, can also provide important clues.

Knowing whether your turtles are male or female is essential for breeding, as well as for providing the proper care they need. For example, females require specific conditions to lay eggs, such as a nesting area with soft soil or sand. By identifying the gender of your turtles, you can create the right environment for their health and reproduction.

BREEDING BEHAVIORS AND CONDITIONS

Spotted turtles usually breed in the spring and early summer, shortly after coming out of their hibernation period. To encourage breeding in captivity, it is important to recreate their natural seasonal changes and provide the right conditions to support healthy mating behavior. Here is how you can prepare for breeding and what to expect during the process.

To prepare for breeding, it is essential to mimic the turtle's natural hibernation cycle. Hibernation plays a key role in stimulating reproduction for spotted turtles. In captivity, you can recreate this by gradually lowering the temperature in their enclosure during the winter months. Keep the temperature between 38-50°F (3-10°C) and allow the turtles to hibernate safely for 2-3 months. During this time, ensure the hibernation area is dark, quiet, and free from disturbances. After the hibernation period, slowly increase the temperature of the enclosure to simulate the arrival of spring, which signals the turtles that it is time to start breeding.

Only healthy, mature turtles should be used for breeding. Spotted turtles typically reach sexual maturity between the ages of 7 and 10 years. Before beginning the breeding process, check that both the male and female turtles are in good health. They should be free of stress, active, and eating a nutritious diet. Healthy turtles are more likely to reproduce successfully and produce healthy offspring.

The enclosure setup also plays a big role in successful breeding. Provide a spacious area with clean water, basking spots, and hiding places. The water in the enclosure should be deep enough for the turtles to swim comfortably but shallow enough for them to reach the surface easily. This will allow the turtles to interact naturally while reducing the risk of stress. A well-maintained environment helps create the conditions needed for breeding.

During the breeding season, you will notice specific mating behaviors, especially from the males. Male spotted turtles become very active and will begin to pursue the females. They may nudge the female's shell, bite her gently, or circle around her in an attempt to get her attention. These behaviors are a normal part of their courtship process.

If the female is receptive, the male will mount her. While mating, the male uses his claws to grip the female's shell to hold himself in place. He aligns his tail with hers to allow for fertilization. Mating can last for several minutes, and it is common for turtles to mate multiple times over the course of a few weeks to ensure successful fertilization.

It is important to monitor the turtles closely during the breeding process. While some level of chasing and nudging is normal, the male can sometimes become too aggressive. If you notice that the female is stressed, injured, or avoiding the male for extended periods, you may need to intervene. In cases of excessive aggression, consider separating the male and female temporarily to allow the female to recover. Once she is ready, you can reintroduce them under supervision.

NESTING AND EGG LAYING

After mating, a female spotted turtle will prepare to lay her eggs. Creating the right conditions for nesting and egg-laying is very important to ensure the eggs develop properly and the hatchlings are healthy.

Recognizing Nesting Behavior

A female turtle getting ready to lay eggs will show clear signs of nesting. She may become more restless, moving around her enclosure and spending extra time on land. You might see her digging in the substrate or searching for a place to lay her eggs. This behavior usually starts a few weeks after mating. It's a signal that she needs a suitable spot to nest.

Preparing a Nesting Area

To help the female lay her eggs, provide a nesting area in the enclosure. Use soft, sandy, or loamy soil where she can easily dig a nest. The soil should be moist but not overly wet; if it's too dry, she may struggle to dig, and if it's too wet, it can harm the eggs. The nesting area should be in a quiet part of the enclosure where she feels safe. Keep the temperature in the nesting area warm, around 80°F (27°C), to mimic the natural conditions she would have in the wild.

When the female finds the right spot, she will start digging a hole using her hind legs. This process can take several hours, as she needs to make the nest deep and safe. Once she lays the eggs, she will carefully cover them with soil to protect them. In captivity, spotted turtles typically lay 2-6 eggs in one clutch.

Collecting and Handling Eggs

If you are breeding turtles in captivity, you can collect the eggs and move them to an incubator to control their conditions. Use clean hands or gloves to handle the eggs gently. Be careful not to rotate or shake the eggs, as this can harm the developing embryos. To keep track of the eggs' position, mark the top of each egg with a pencil before moving them.

Incubating the Eggs

Place the eggs in a container filled with a moist substrate, such as vermiculite or perlite. The substrate should hold moisture well, as the eggs need a humid environment to develop properly. Keep the humidity level at 70-80%, and monitor it regularly to ensure it stays consistent.

The ideal temperature for incubation is between 82-86°F (28-30°C). The temperature not only affects how quickly the eggs hatch but also influences the gender of the hatchlings. Higher temperatures (around 86°F) result in more females, while lower temperatures (closer to 82°F) produce more males. Use a thermometer to check the temperature in the incubator and adjust it if needed.

The eggs usually take 60-90 days to hatch, depending on the temperature and humidity. During this time, avoid disturbing the eggs unless necessary. Too much movement or handling can harm the embryos.

Caring for Hatchlings

When the eggs are ready to hatch, the baby turtles, called hatchlings, will emerge from their shells. You'll notice a small yolk sac attached to their underside. This sac provides the nutrients they need for the first few days, so it's important to avoid touching or handling them excessively during this time.

Place the hatchlings in a shallow water enclosure where they can swim easily but still reach the surface to breathe. The water should be clean and warm, with plenty of hiding places and aquatic plants to make them feel secure. Provide a basking area with access to heat and UVB lighting to support their growth and development.

Hatchlings need a diet rich in protein to help them grow. Offer them small insects, worms, and other high-protein foods. As they grow, you can start to include more plant-based foods to balance their diet.

Chapter 9

PREPARING AN INCUBATION SETUP

To successfully incubate spotted turtle eggs, you need to create a setup that mimics the natural conditions required for the eggs to develop. This setup helps keep the eggs safe, moist, and at the right temperature during the incubation period. Proper care and attention at this stage are essential for healthy hatchlings.

When the female turtle lays her eggs, the first step is to collect them carefully. Start by locating the nest, which will likely be in a quiet area with soft soil. Once you find the eggs, gently dig them out without rotating or shaking them. This is very important because moving the eggs from their original position can harm the developing embryos inside. To help you keep track of their orientation, use a pencil to lightly mark the top of each egg. After marking them, move the eggs to a prepared container or incubator.

Next, you'll need to select or build a suitable incubator. A commercial reptile egg incubator is a great choice because it is specifically designed to maintain the stable temperature and humidity levels needed for successful incubation. If you don't have access to a commercial incubator, you can make a simple DIY version. For this, you'll need a plastic container with a secure lid, a reliable heat source, and tools like a thermometer and a hygrometer to monitor the temperature and humidity. Whether you use a commercial or DIY incubator, the goal is to create a controlled environment where the eggs can develop without any disturbances.

Once you have an incubator ready, the next step is to prepare the substrate, which acts as the bedding for the eggs. Vermiculite and perlite are excellent choices for this purpose because they retain moisture while allowing air to circulate around the eggs. To prepare the substrate, mix it with water in a ratio of one part water to one part substrate by weight. For example, if you're using 100 grams of vermiculite, add 100 grams of water. The substrate should feel moist but not soggy. If there's too much water, it can block air from reaching the eggs, which can suffocate the embryos.

After preparing the substrate, carefully place the eggs into the container. Make sure each egg is partially buried in the moist substrate but not completely covered. The eggs need some exposure to air, so leave the tops visible. Space the eggs apart so they don't touch each other. This spacing allows proper air circulation and ensures that if one egg develops problems, it won't affect the others. Once the eggs are in place, close the lid of the incubation container. Don't seal the lid tightly; it's important to allow some air exchange to maintain oxygen flow while keeping the humidity levels high.

Inside the incubator, monitor the temperature and humidity regularly to ensure they stay within the ideal range. For spotted turtle eggs, the temperature should be between 82 and 86°F (28 to 30°C), and the humidity should stay around 70-80%. Use a thermometer and hygrometer to check these levels daily, and adjust the incubator settings if needed. Keeping the conditions stable throughout the incubation period will give the eggs the best chance of developing properly.

MONITORING TEMPERATURE AND HUMIDITY

Maintaining the correct temperature and humidity is essential for spotted turtle eggs to develop properly during incubation. Even small changes in these conditions can affect the success of hatching and may also influence whether the hatchlings are male or female. Proper monitoring ensures the best chances of healthy development.

To begin, it's important to keep the temperature in the right range. The ideal temperature for incubating spotted turtle eggs is between 82°F and 86°F (28°C to 30°C). This range is perfect for the embryos to grow and develop. If the temperature is on the lower end, around 82°F, the hatchlings are more likely to be male. On the other hand, higher temperatures closer to 86°F will result in more female hatchlings. However, it is crucial to avoid temperatures below 77°F (25°C) or above 90°F (32°C), as these can harm or even kill the developing embryos. Using a reliable thermometer to monitor the temperature inside the incubator is vital. Check the thermometer every day to ensure the temperature stays steady.

Equally important is maintaining the right level of humidity, as spotted turtle eggs need a moist environment to develop. The humidity level should remain between 70% and 80% throughout the incubation process. To achieve this, the substrate (such as vermiculite or perlite) should be kept moist but not soaking wet. Check the substrate regularly by feeling its texture; it should be slightly damp but not soggy. If the substrate begins to dry out, add water carefully. The best method is to drip water around the edges of the container instead of pouring it directly onto the eggs, which could harm the embryos. Using a hygrometer to measure the humidity level is very helpful, as it provides an accurate reading. Check the hygrometer daily along with the temperature.

Monitoring and adjusting these conditions consistently is key to a successful incubation process. Check both the temperature and humidity every day to ensure they stay within the correct range. If there are any changes, make adjustments immediately. For example, if the temperature drops, you can increase the heat source slightly. If the humidity falls below the desired level, you can add a small amount of water to the substrate. Keep the incubator in a stable location, away from direct sunlight, drafts, or sources of vibration. Excessive movement or sudden changes in the environment can disrupt the eggs' development. Also, avoid opening the incubation container too often, as this can cause fluctuations in temperature and humidity inside.

The incubation period for spotted turtle eggs usually lasts between 60 and 90 days, depending on the temperature. Warmer temperatures tend to shorten the incubation time, while cooler temperatures may extend it. As the eggs near the hatching date, you may notice signs of development. Look for tiny cracks forming on the eggshells or slight movement inside the eggs. These are indications that the hatchlings are getting ready to emerge. Be patient and avoid disturbing the eggs during this critical time.

CARING FOR HATCHLINGS

When spotted turtle eggs hatch, the baby turtles, called hatchlings, need special care to ensure they grow healthy and strong. The first few weeks of their life are very important, and providing a safe and nurturing environment is key to their survival.

The hatching process begins when the baby turtles are ready to come out of their eggs. They use a small, temporary structure on their snout, called an egg tooth, to crack open the eggshell. This process can take time, so it's best to let the hatchlings emerge on their own. Avoid helping them unless they are struggling or the eggshell is unusually thick. Interfering too much can harm the delicate hatchlings.

When the baby turtles first hatch, they will have a small yolk sac attached to their underside. This yolk sac is full of nutrients and provides food for the hatchlings during their first few days of life. It is important not to touch or disturb the yolk sac, as it is essential for their development. Place the hatchlings in a shallow container with a moist paper towel or soft substrate, like damp sphagnum moss, to protect the yolk sac from injury. The yolk sac will shrink and be absorbed into their body within 2 to 5 days.

Once the yolk sac is fully absorbed, the hatchlings are ready to move to a small aquatic enclosure. The enclosure should have clean, dechlorinated water that is shallow enough for the baby turtles to stand in without difficulty. A good rule of thumb is to make the water no deeper than the height of the hatchling's shell to prevent accidental drowning. Add smooth rocks or platforms so the hatchlings can climb out of the water to bask. Including aquatic plants and small hiding spots will make the enclosure feel safe and natural for them.

Hatchlings need proper lighting and temperature to stay healthy. Provide a basking area with a temperature of around 85°F (29°C) where they can warm themselves. UVB lighting is essential, as it helps their bodies produce vitamin D3, which is needed for strong shells and bones. The water temperature should be kept between 75°F and 80°F (24°C to 27°C), which you can achieve using a submersible aquarium heater. Check the temperatures regularly to ensure the environment remains stable.

Feeding hatchlings begins once the yolk sac has been fully absorbed. At this stage, they need a diet rich in protein to support their rapid growth. Offer them small, easy-to-eat foods like pinhead crickets, finely chopped earthworms, mealworms, and commercial turtle pellets designed for hatchlings. Over time, introduce small amounts of vegetables, such as finely shredded leafy greens like dandelion greens, collard greens, or kale. This will help them get used to a balanced diet as they grow older.

It's important to monitor the hatchlings closely for signs of good health and growth. Watch for any issues such as lethargy, swelling, or problems with their shells. Regularly clean their enclosure to remove waste and uneaten food, as a dirty environment can lead to infections and illnesses. Provide fresh water daily to keep their habitat clean and healthy.

Chapter 10

SPECIAL HOUSING NEEDS FOR YOUNG TURTLES

Young turtles, especially hatchlings and juveniles, need a carefully designed environment that supports their growth, safety, and overall well-being. The right setup can help them thrive and reduce stress, while also minimizing the risk of injury. Here's how to create a suitable habitat for young turtles.

First, you need to choose the right size enclosure. Hatchlings are small, so they should be kept in a tank or container that is just the right size for them. A 10-20 gallon tank is usually sufficient for one or two hatchlings. As the turtles grow and become more active, you can upgrade to a larger tank to give them more space to swim and bask comfortably. Overcrowding should be avoided because it can stress the turtles and lead to health problems.

Water depth is another important consideration. Hatchlings are not strong swimmers and should not be in deep water. Too much water could lead to drowning, so it's important to keep the water shallow. For very young turtles, a water depth of around 1-2 inches (2.5-5 cm) is ideal. This allows them to stand on the bottom and easily reach the surface for air. As the turtles grow and become better swimmers, you can gradually increase the depth to allow more room for swimming.

A basking area is also essential for young turtles. Turtles need to bask to dry off and warm up. The basking spot should allow them to completely dry their shells and get some heat to regulate their body temperature. Smooth rocks, pieces of driftwood, or commercial basking platforms work well for creating a safe and stable basking area. The surface should be easily accessible to the turtles so they can climb out of the water without difficulty.

When setting up lighting and temperature, it's important to create an environment that mimics natural conditions. Young turtles need a basking area with a temperature between 85-90°F (29-32°C). The water temperature should be kept between 75-80°F (24-27°C). A UVB light is also a must, as it provides the ultraviolet radiation that turtles need for proper calcium absorption and shell development. Place the UVB light above the basking area and leave it on for 10-12 hours each day. This will help your turtles stay healthy and promote their growth.

Another important feature is providing hiding spots and decorations in the enclosure. Hiding spots are crucial for helping the turtles feel safe and secure. Live or artificial plants, small caves, or pieces of driftwood can serve as hiding spots both in the water and on land. These decorations also add enrichment to the enclosure, making it more interesting for the turtles. A well-structured enclosure helps them feel less stressed and more comfortable in their environment.

Finally, clean water is essential for maintaining the health of young turtles. Always use dechlorinated water to avoid harmful chemicals that can irritate their skin and eyes. A gentle filter is useful for maintaining water quality without creating strong currents that might make it harder for the turtles to swim. It's also important to perform partial water changes every week and clean the tank regularly to ensure the water stays fresh and free from bacteria and waste.

DIETARY REQUIREMENTS FOR GROWTH

Young spotted turtles need a well-balanced diet to support their rapid growth. Since they are still developing, their dietary needs are different from those of adult turtles. They require more protein and other nutrients during their early life stages. Here is an overview of the key components of their diet.

Protein is the most important part of a hatchling's diet. Young spotted turtles are primarily carnivores, and they thrive on high-quality animal protein. You can offer small insects, like pinhead crickets, fruit flies, and tiny mealworms. These are great sources of protein and other essential nutrients. You can also feed them finely chopped earthworms or bloodworms, which are soft and easy to eat for young turtles. Additionally, there are commercial turtle pellets designed specifically for juvenile turtles, which can be a convenient option to ensure a balanced diet. These pellets often contain the right mix of protein, fats, and other necessary nutrients.

As the turtles grow, you can start to gradually introduce plant-based foods into their diet. Although young turtles need a lot of protein, offering some vegetables and aquatic plants is important for their long-term health. Shredded leafy greens such as kale, collard greens, and dandelion greens are excellent choices. These greens are rich in vitamins and minerals that help support their overall health. You can also offer aquatic plants like duckweed, water lettuce, or elodea. These plants provide fiber and other nutrients that are important for the turtle's digestion and general well-being. As the turtles mature, the amount of plant-based foods in their diet can increase, but protein should still remain the main component.

In addition to protein and vegetables, calcium is a critical part of a young turtle's diet. Calcium helps support strong shell and bone development. Without enough calcium, the turtle's shell can become soft and malformed. To ensure that the turtle gets enough calcium, you can provide a calcium supplement. Dusting the live food (like insects or worms) or vegetables with calcium powder is a good way to add it to their diet. You should use a calcium powder that is free from phosphorus, as too much phosphorus can interfere with calcium absorption. It is recommended to supplement their diet with calcium once or twice a week.

Along with calcium, vitamins are also important for the turtle's growth and health. A multivitamin supplement designed for reptiles can help fill in any nutritional gaps in the diet. These vitamins are crucial for boosting the immune system and supporting the turtle's overall development. It's best to provide the multivitamin once a week to ensure they are getting the right amount of vitamins, especially if they are not getting a diverse range of foods. Be sure to follow the instructions on the supplement to avoid over-supplementation.

When it comes to feeding, hatchlings should be fed daily. Offer small amounts of food that they can consume within 10 to 15 minutes. This allows the turtles to eat enough without overfeeding, which can lead to water quality problems. Make sure to remove any uneaten food promptly to prevent it from polluting the water. A clean feeding environment is essential for the health of your turtles, as decaying food can lead to harmful bacteria and infections.

In terms of hydration, turtles get most of the water they need from their enclosure. It's important to provide them with access to clean, fresh water at all times. Young turtles are still growing and need adequate hydration for healthy shell development and digestion. Ensure that the water in the enclosure is changed regularly, and make sure that the water is free from chlorine, as chlorine can be harmful to turtles.

PREVENTING ILLNESS IN HATCHLINGS

Hatchlings and young turtles are more susceptible to illness than adult turtles. It's important to keep them healthy by maintaining a clean environment, providing the right food, and watching for signs of stress or illness. Here are some tips for preventing common health problems in hatchlings.

First and foremost, keeping the enclosure clean is essential. Poor water quality is one of the main causes of illness in young turtles. Turtles produce waste that can pollute their water, so it's important to regularly check the water parameters and clean the enclosure. Remove any uneaten food, waste, or debris from the tank to keep the water clear. Using a good filter can also help maintain water quality, but regular cleaning and water changes are still necessary to keep things hygienic.

Another key to preventing illness is monitoring the turtles for signs of stress or sickness. Some symptoms to watch for include lethargy, loss of appetite, swollen or cloudy eyes, shell deformities or discoloration, difficulty swimming, or irregular breathing. If you notice any of these signs, it's important to consult a reptile veterinarian right away. Early treatment can prevent small issues from becoming bigger problems.

It's also important not to overcrowd the enclosure. When hatchlings are housed in close quarters, they can experience stress, and this can lead to competition for food and space. Each turtle needs enough room to move around, bask, and hide when they want to feel safe. Overcrowding can increase the risk of injury, stress, and illness. Make sure the tank is large enough for the number of turtles you have, and consider upgrading to a larger enclosure as they grow.

Shell infections are another concern for young turtles. Hatchlings are especially vulnerable to fungal and bacterial infections, particularly if their environment is too wet or dirty. To prevent these infections, provide a basking area where the turtles can dry off completely each day. Drying off helps them maintain healthy shells and prevents moisture from accumulating in places where bacteria or fungi can thrive. Keeping the water clean and making sure there is a proper basking spot can go a long way in preventing shell infections.

Handling young turtles should be kept to a minimum to reduce stress and prevent injuries. Turtles, especially hatchlings, can easily become stressed by excessive handling, and this can affect their health. If you must handle your turtle, make sure to use clean, wet hands to gently support the turtle. Avoid dropping or handling them roughly, as this can cause injury. Try to limit handling to only when absolutely necessary, such as during health checks or tank cleaning.

Proper lighting is crucial for preventing health issues in young turtles. UVB light helps them absorb calcium and supports healthy shell growth. Without UVB lighting, hatchlings can develop metabolic bone disease, a condition that affects their bones and shells. To prevent this, ensure that your turtles have access to a UVB light source. Be sure to replace the UVB bulb every 6 to 12 months, as its effectiveness decreases over time. Keeping the right lighting in their environment is vital for their growth and health.

Lastly, regular veterinary checkups are important for monitoring the health of your hatchlings. A reptile veterinarian can perform health assessments, check for parasites, and ensure that your turtles are growing properly. Regular vet visits help catch any health problems early, which can make treatment more effective. Early detection of issues like infections, vitamin deficiencies, or shell problems can prevent them from becoming more serious.

Chapter 11

COMMON DISEASES AND THEIR PREVENTION

S potted turtles, like all reptiles, can develop certain diseases that affect their health. Recognizing symptoms early and taking the right preventive measures can help avoid many of these issues. Here are some common diseases spotted turtles may face, along with ways to prevent them.

One of the most common health issues is respiratory infections. These infections can show up as symptoms like wheezing, coughing, nasal discharge, or difficulty breathing. Respiratory infections are often caused by poor water quality, improper humidity, or cold temperatures. To prevent these problems, it is important to maintain a clean environment. Keep the water temperature between 75-80°F (24-27°C) and ensure that basking areas are heated to 85-90°F (29-32°C). Avoid drafts and make sure the humidity levels are appropriate. Keeping the habitat clean and at the right temperature can go a long way in preventing respiratory infections.

Shell rot is another serious condition that affects spotted turtles. Symptoms of shell rot include soft or discolored patches on the shell, a foul smell, and swelling. This condition is usually caused by bacterial or fungal infections, which are often linked to dirty water or damp living conditions. To prevent shell rot, it's essential to maintain a clean environment for the turtle. Providing a dry basking area helps reduce excessive moisture, which can contribute to shell rot. Additionally, cleaning the turtle's shell gently with a soft cloth or sponge can help remove dirt or debris without causing damage. Avoid scrubbing the shell too hard, as this can harm it.

Metabolic Bone Disease (MBD) is another condition that affects spotted turtles, particularly young ones. MBD causes symptoms such as soft or deformed shells, difficulty moving, tremors, or lethargy. This condition is caused by a lack of calcium or improper UVB lighting, which prevents the turtle from absorbing calcium properly. To prevent MBD, it is important to provide a balanced diet rich in calcium. Make sure the turtle has access to proper UVB lighting, which should be placed above the basking area and be on for 10-12 hours each day. In addition to UVB lighting, consider supplementing the turtle's diet with calcium powder or providing cuttlebone, which is a natural source of calcium.

Eye infections are another common issue in turtles. Symptoms include swollen or cloudy eyes, discharge, or difficulty opening the eyes. Eye infections are usually caused by poor water quality, lack of UVB light, or injury. To prevent eye infections, maintain clean water and proper lighting. Regularly check the turtle's eyes for any signs of swelling or irritation. If the eyes remain closed for a prolonged period or show signs of infection, seek veterinary care immediately. Preventing eye infections is often as simple as keeping the turtle's habitat clean and providing the right lighting.

Infections and abscesses are another health concern for spotted turtles. Symptoms of these infections include swelling or lumps under the skin, typically around the neck or limbs. These lumps are often associated with bacterial infections. Infections can occur from wounds, bites, or poor hygiene. To prevent infections and abscesses, always handle turtles gently to avoid causing injury. It's also important to keep their living area free of sharp objects that could lead to cuts or scrapes. Maintaining good hygiene in their habitat, including regularly cleaning the enclosure and removing waste, helps minimize the risk of infections.

PARASITE MANAGEMENT

Parasites are a common health concern for spotted turtles and can be either external or internal. These parasites can harm the turtle's health, so it's important to know how to recognize the symptoms and take preventive measures.

External parasites include mites or ticks, which can cause visible irritation, scratching, or unusual behavior in the turtle. These parasites often come from contact with other animals or from an unclean environment. To prevent external parasites, it's essential to keep the turtle's enclosure clean. Regularly check your turtle for signs of mites or ticks, which can appear as small bumps or scabs on the skin. If you notice any signs of external parasites, it is best to consult a veterinarian. The vet may recommend safe treatments, such as a topical solution or a bath in an antiseptic solution, to eliminate the parasites.

Internal parasites, such as roundworms or tapeworms, can also be a problem for spotted turtles. Symptoms of internal parasites include weight loss, diarrhea, lethargy, or abnormal stool. These parasites are typically contracted from contaminated water or food. To prevent internal parasites, make sure your turtle is fed clean, properly prepared food, and avoid feeding wild-caught insects, which may carry parasites. Always provide clean, filtered water to your turtle, as this can help prevent the spread of parasites. Additionally, regular deworming under the guidance of a veterinarian can help prevent or treat internal parasites. If you notice any unusual symptoms like weight loss or diarrhea, consult a vet for a fecal examination to check for internal parasites.

Fungal infections are another potential issue for spotted turtles, especially if their living environment is too damp or unsanitary. Symptoms of a fungal infection include white patches or a fluffy appearance on the skin or shell. Fungal infections thrive in humid, wet conditions, so it's important to maintain proper humidity levels in the turtle's enclosure. Ensure that your turtle has access to a dry basking area where it can completely dry off each day. This will help prevent fungal growth. If you notice any white patches or unusual changes in your turtle's appearance, consult a veterinarian for proper antifungal treatment. Fungal infections are treatable, but it's important to act quickly to prevent them from spreading or worsening.

In addition to these specific parasite concerns, regular health checks are essential for overall parasite management. Regularly inspect your turtle for any signs of external or internal parasites. Check for visible signs of irritation, changes in behavior, or any symptoms such as diarrhea or weight loss. Maintaining a clean and dry environment is crucial, as it helps prevent the growth of harmful parasites and bacteria. Cleaning the turtle's enclosure regularly and changing the water frequently will reduce the risk of parasite outbreaks.

If you suspect that your turtle may have a parasitic infection, it's important to take it to a veterinarian. A vet can perform a fecal examination to check for internal parasites and provide treatment if needed. A veterinarian can also offer advice on how to prevent parasites and maintain the turtle's health. Regular vet checkups are a good way to ensure that your turtle remains healthy and free of parasites.

WHEN TO SEEK VETERINARY CARE

Even with the best care, there may be times when your spotted turtle needs to see a veterinarian. Knowing when to seek professional help is important to ensure the health and well-being of your turtle. Here are some signs to watch for, which may indicate it's time for veterinary care.

If your turtle shows persistent symptoms like lethargy, a lack of appetite, abnormal breathing, or discharge that doesn't improve after a few days, it's time to consult a veterinarian. These could be signs of a more serious condition, such as an infection or a metabolic problem, which requires medical treatment. For example, if your turtle is not eating for an extended period or seems very tired and weak, it could indicate a health issue that needs professional attention. Similarly, if your turtle is having trouble breathing, has nasal discharge, or any other unusual symptoms that don't go away, a veterinarian can help determine what's wrong and provide appropriate treatment.

Another situation where you should seek veterinary care is if your turtle has an injury. This can include a crack or fracture in the shell, bleeding, swelling, or any signs of trauma. A shell fracture is especially serious, as it can lead to infection if not treated correctly. In such cases, it's important to get your turtle to a vet immediately so they can clean the wound, treat any infection, and take steps to ensure proper healing. Injury to the shell or other parts of the body can lead to complications if not properly managed, so timely care is essential.

Spotted turtles shed their skin and scutes (the outer layers of their shell) regularly. However, sometimes a turtle may have difficulty shedding, and this can cause problems. If you notice that your turtle has retained skin or scutes that are not coming off naturally, it could lead to irritation or infection. A veterinarian can help with this issue by either offering treatment or providing advice on how to assist the turtle in shedding its skin and scutes. This is especially important because retained scutes or skin can become infected and cause further health issues if left untreated.

If your turtle shows sudden changes in behavior, it could also be a sign that something is wrong. For example, if your turtle becomes very aggressive, overly shy, or shows erratic behavior that is not typical for them, it could indicate stress, pain, or illness. Behavioral changes are often one of the first signs of an underlying health issue. A veterinarian can help identify the cause of the behavior change and recommend appropriate treatment or changes to the turtle's environment to reduce stress and help them feel better.

Lastly, even if your turtle seems healthy, regular veterinary checkups are a good idea. Just like people, turtles benefit from routine exams to ensure they are healthy and to catch potential issues before they become serious. A reptile-savvy veterinarian can check your turtle's overall health, perform fecal tests for parasites, and assess the condition of the shell. These checkups can help identify any problems early on, giving your turtle the best chance at a long and healthy life. Regular checkups are especially important as your turtle ages, as they may become more susceptible to health issues over time.

Chapter 12

UNDERSTANDING BRUMATION IN SPOTTED TURTLES

B
rumation is a special process that turtles, including spotted turtles, go through during the colder months. It's similar to hibernation, but it works a little differently for reptiles. Unlike mammals that go into a deep sleep during winter, brumation is a lighter, slower state where the turtle's body slows down, but it doesn't completely stop. This allows the turtle to conserve energy when the weather is cold, and food is harder to find.

During brumation, a spotted turtle's metabolism slows down a lot. This means their body processes, like digestion, slow down, and they don't need as much food or water. In fact, many turtles won't eat at all during brumation. Their activity level drops significantly, and they might stay hidden or very still for long periods. This is a natural part of their cycle that helps them survive the colder months when it is harder to find food.

The process of brumation is heavily influenced by temperature. Turtles are cold-blooded animals, which means they depend on external temperatures to regulate their body heat. When the environmental temperature drops below a certain point, usually between 50°F and 60°F (10-15°C), spotted turtles will begin brumating. This means that as the weather gets colder, their bodies naturally slow down, and they enter this period of reduced activity. When the temperature begins to rise again, their metabolism picks up, and they wake up from brumation.

Brumation can last for different amounts of time. Typically, it lasts for several weeks, but it can extend to a few months depending on how cold it is and the individual turtle's health. The turtle's overall condition, including its size, age, and the amount of fat reserves it has, can affect how long it stays in this slow state.

In the wild, brumation helps turtles survive harsh winters when food is scarce, and the weather is too cold to remain active. However, in captivity, brumation can be influenced by the temperature in the turtle's enclosure. If the temperature drops to the right level, the turtle may enter brumation on its own. This means that if you are keeping a spotted turtle as a pet, you should be mindful of the temperature in its enclosure to ensure it's appropriate for the turtle's natural brumation cycle.

It's important to understand how brumation works because it impacts your turtle's care. When your turtle is brumating, it will need very little food and water. You should not try to force it to eat or drink, as it is not necessary for its survival during this time. However, if you notice that your turtle is showing signs of illness or distress during brumation, it is important to consult a veterinarian to make sure there is not an underlying problem.

Some spotted turtles may not brumate every year, depending on their age, health, and the conditions in their environment. For example, younger turtles or turtles that are not in the best health may not brumate, while older, healthier turtles may enter brumation more regularly. You should observe your turtle's behavior carefully to understand whether it is entering brumation and ensure it has a safe and suitable environment for this process.

PREPARING FOR WINTER BRUMATION

Preparing your spotted turtle for brumation is important to ensure that it safely goes through this resting period. Brumation is a natural process for turtles, but you need to take steps to make sure your turtle is ready. By creating the right environment and checking the turtle's health, you can help ensure it enters brumation in good condition.

The first thing to do before allowing your turtle to enter brumation is to check its health. Make sure that your turtle is in good health, without signs of illness. Look for any changes in behavior, like being unusually sleepy, not eating, or acting abnormally. If your turtle shows signs of illness, it's best to delay brumation until it gets better. You should also make sure your turtle is well-fed and hydrated before it starts brumation. A healthy, well-nourished turtle is more likely to handle brumation successfully, so it's important to give it the proper care leading up to this time.

Brumation is very dependent on temperature, so it's important to adjust the temperature in your turtle's enclosure gradually. The temperature should not drop suddenly, as this could stress your turtle. Start by lowering the temperature slowly over a few weeks. You can begin around 70°F (21°C) and gradually reduce it to around 50-60°F (10-15°C), which is the typical temperature range that triggers brumation. This gradual drop helps your turtle's body adjust to the change and prepares it for the slower, more restful state of brumation.

You also need to provide a suitable environment for your turtle during brumation. If you are planning to let your turtle brumate indoors, it should be placed in a cool, quiet spot away from bright light, drafts, and noise. A place like a basement or a cool room that stays quiet and undisturbed is ideal. If your turtle is kept outdoors in a pond or an outdoor enclosure, make sure the pond is deep enough to prevent the water from freezing completely. This will allow your turtle to bury itself in the substrate and stay safe during the colder months. It's important that the temperature is not too warm in the brumation area. If the space is too warm, your turtle may not enter brumation, and it could become stressed. Make sure the environment is just cool enough for it to rest properly.

As brumation approaches, you should start to reduce the amount of food you offer your turtle. In the weeks leading up to brumation, turtles often lose interest in food, so it's best not to force them to eat. About 1-2 weeks before the brumation period, stop feeding your turtle entirely. This allows its digestive system to empty out, which is important because food that is left in the stomach could start to ferment while the turtle is inactive. If food ferments, it could cause infections or other health issues. Letting your turtle's digestive system rest helps avoid these problems.

During brumation, humidity levels should be kept low. Brumation is usually a dry process, so it's important to monitor the humidity in the area where your turtle is resting. If you are keeping your turtle indoors, make sure that the space is not too moist. Excess humidity can lead to mold or fungal growth, which can harm your turtle. Make sure the brumation environment is dry enough to prevent these issues while still allowing your turtle to rest comfortably.

POST-BRUMATION CARE

Once the cold weather begins to ease and the temperatures rise again, your spotted turtle will start to wake up from brumation. After a long period of dormancy, it's important to support your turtle as it transitions back to its normal activity. This process must be handled carefully to ensure your turtle remains healthy and comfortable.

The first thing to do after brumation is to gradually warm the enclosure. Rapid temperature changes can shock your turtle's system, so it's important to bring the temperature back up slowly. Start by adjusting the water temperature to the normal range of 75-80°F (24-27°C), and make sure the basking area is around 85-90°F (29-32°C). If you had used artificial heating during brumation, you should remove the heating elements slowly to allow a steady increase in temperature. This gradual warming helps your turtle adjust comfortably and reduces the risk of stress.

Next, it's time to reintroduce food, but you should do so slowly. After weeks or months without eating, your turtle may not be very hungry when it first wakes up. Start by offering small amounts of food to stimulate its appetite. Begin with easily digestible foods such as insects, chopped fruits, and leafy greens. This helps ease your turtle back into its regular feeding routine. Keep an eye on your turtle's eating habits, and ensure it starts eating normally within one to two weeks. If your turtle doesn't eat after this period, it's a good idea to consult a veterinarian for further advice.

Even though your turtle may not have eaten during brumation, it is crucial to make sure it has access to fresh water right away. Brumation can lead to dehydration, so offering clean, fresh water is important for rehydrating your turtle as it wakes up. Provide the water in shallow containers to make it easy for your turtle to access. Make sure the water is clean and free of any contaminants to avoid any health issues.

As your turtle begins to eat and move around again, it's important to carefully monitor its behavior. Watch for any signs that may indicate it's having trouble adjusting. If your turtle appears lethargic, or if you notice symptoms like swelling, discharge from the eyes or nose, or irregular shell growth, it could indicate an underlying health problem. If you see any unusual symptoms, it's essential to consult a veterinarian immediately to get the proper care and treatment.

Your turtle's behavior will gradually improve as it becomes more active. It will start to swim, bask, and feed more regularly. However, during this time, it's important to keep a close watch on its health and wellbeing. Make sure it is fully transitioning back to its normal routine. Once your turtle is fully awake, active, and eating well, you can resume your usual care routine for the warmer months. This includes maintaining the proper temperature, providing fresh food and water, and ensuring it has the right amount of space to swim, bask, and hide.

Chapter 13

PROVIDING MENTAL STIMULATION

Mental stimulation is important for the health and well-being of spotted turtles. In the wild, they engage in many activities that help keep their minds active, such as searching for food, exploring their environment, and interacting with other turtles. In captivity, it's essential to provide opportunities for them to engage in these natural behaviors and keep their minds sharp.

One way to provide mental stimulation is by offering foraging opportunities. In the wild, spotted turtles spend a lot of time foraging for food. They look for aquatic plants, insects, and small invertebrates. To replicate this behavior in captivity, you can hide their food in different places around their enclosure. For example, you can scatter their food across the area, bury it in the substrate, or place it inside floating containers. This encourages the turtle to search for its food, much like it would in the wild. Another way to keep them engaged is by offering a variety of food that they have to "hunt" for. You can place live insects or small pieces of fruits and vegetables in the water, challenging the turtle to use its senses of sight and smell to locate and catch its food. This keeps them mentally active and stimulates their natural foraging instincts.

Turtles are also naturally curious and enjoy exploring their surroundings. To provide them with mental stimulation, it's a good idea to give them an enclosure that encourages exploration. If possible, you can offer a larger or more complex space where the turtle can move around and discover new areas.

Including both land and water areas in the enclosure allows them to engage in more varied behaviors, such as swimming, basking, and hiding. Adding plants, rocks, and logs to the enclosure can create natural hiding spots where the turtle can explore and feel secure. By making the environment more interesting and varied, you help keep your turtle engaged and encourage natural behaviors like climbing, hiding, and swimming.

Creating different levels within the enclosure can also encourage exploration. You can add ramps, platforms, or submerged areas to the setup. This makes the environment more dynamic and allows the turtle to move between different levels, mimicking the variety of terrain it would encounter in its natural habitat. By providing these types of opportunities, you help prevent boredom and encourage your turtle to explore and interact with its environment in a way that feels more natural.

Although spotted turtles are solitary animals by nature, they do interact with other turtles in the wild, especially during the breeding season or when basking. In captivity, if you have more than one turtle, they may enjoy some social interaction. Allowing turtles to share space can provide some social stimulation, but it is important to monitor them closely. Spotted turtles can sometimes become aggressive or stressed if they feel their space is being invaded or if they are competing for resources like food or basking spots. It's essential to ensure that each turtle has enough space and that resources are provided in such a way that there is no competition. If you notice signs of aggression or stress, it might be necessary to separate the turtles or adjust the environment to reduce tension.

TOYS AND INTERACTIVE FEATURES FOR TURTLES

While turtles don't play with toys the way mammals or birds might, they can still enjoy and benefit from certain items and features that provide interaction and mental challenges. Interactive toys and objects can help stimulate their curiosity and encourage healthy, active behaviors.

One type of interactive feature that can engage your turtle is floating objects. Floating items like logs, small rafts, or platforms can give your turtle something to interact with in the water. Some turtles enjoy swimming around these objects or climbing onto them to bask in the sun. These objects also help your turtle practice its swimming and climbing skills. You can try different materials, such as cork or smooth wood, to see what your turtle prefers. Some turtles might also enjoy pushing around floating toys like small rubber balls or plastic items. However, you should be careful to avoid any toys that could break into small pieces that your turtle could swallow, as this could be harmful.

Another way to provide mental stimulation for your turtle is by offering hide boxes and shelters. Spotted turtles are often shy creatures that like to have a place to retreat when they feel stressed or just need some privacy. By providing small shelters made from safe materials like plastic or wood, you can give your turtle a safe and secure space to hide. Placing a hide box near the basking area allows your turtle to retreat to a cozy spot after warming up. Alternatively, placing the hide box near the water provides your turtle with a sense of security while swimming. These shelters offer your turtle a private space and can help reduce stress, which is an important part of keeping your turtle healthy and happy.

Puzzle feeders are another great way to engage your turtle mentally. These types of feeders or treat-dispensing toys are designed to challenge your turtle during feeding time. You can fill them with your turtle's favorite treats, and your turtle will need to figure out how to open or manipulate the toy to access the food inside. Puzzle feeders encourage problem-solving and mimic natural behaviors, such as foraging for food. They provide an enriching challenge that can keep your turtle entertained and mentally stimulated. Introducing food puzzles to your turtle's routine can add variety to its diet while also promoting healthy mental exercise.

Live plants can also be a valuable addition to your turtle's enclosure, offering both aesthetic appeal and interactive features. Adding live plants helps to mimic the turtle's natural environment and provides a stimulating area for exploration. Your turtle may nibble on the plants, explore them, or use them as cover. Floating aquatic plants, such as duckweed or water lilies, provide hiding spots for your turtle and encourage it to explore its surroundings. Land-based plants also give your turtle a natural environment to climb on or hide in. When adding live plants, it's important to choose ones that are safe and non-toxic for turtles, as some plants can be harmful if ingested. Check that the plants are suitable for your turtle's enclosure before introducing them.

By adding floating objects, hide boxes, puzzle feeders, and live plants, you can provide your spotted turtle with various ways to engage its mind and body. These features not only help to replicate the natural environment of a turtle but also encourage exploration, problem-solving, and mental stimulation.

PREVENTING BOREDOM IN CAPTIVE SPOTTED TURTLES

Boredom can be harmful to turtles, leading to stress and potential health issues. To keep your spotted turtle happy and healthy, it's important to provide an environment filled with opportunities for stimulation. This helps to prevent boredom and ensures that your turtle remains active, mentally engaged, and physically healthy.

One way to prevent boredom is by adding variety to the environment. You can change the layout of your turtle's enclosure by rotating objects like logs, rocks, and basking spots. This provides a new challenge and helps to keep the environment interesting. You can also rearrange plants and hiding spots, giving your turtle a fresh landscape to explore. This change in scenery can prevent your turtle from becoming accustomed to the same surroundings, which might otherwise lead to boredom.

In addition to moving objects around, you can also swap out different substrates like sand, pebbles, or coconut coir. These materials offer different textures for your turtle to interact with and dig into, mimicking its natural environment. Turtles are naturally curious, and having different textures to explore can keep them mentally stimulated. The more variety you provide, the more engaging the environment becomes for your turtle.

Regular interaction is another important way to keep your turtle engaged. While turtles are not typically affectionate animals, they can become familiar with their caretaker and develop a sense of comfort. Gently interacting with your turtle can help reduce feelings of boredom. You can engage with your turtle during feeding time or when you allow it to explore outside of its enclosure in a safe, controlled area. Simply spending time near your turtle and allowing it to become familiar with your presence can help reduce any stress it might feel from isolation.

If you want to add another level of interaction, you can train your turtle to respond to certain stimuli. For example, tapping on the enclosure before feeding time or providing a special signal can help your turtle recognize the routine and add an interactive element to its day. This small form of training can also help strengthen the bond between you and your turtle, as it becomes more accustomed to your presence and activities.

Environmental challenges are another way to keep your turtle mentally engaged. Adding obstacles to the enclosure, such as creating shallow water areas with rocks or sticks, can encourage your turtle to navigate through or around them. These small challenges stimulate your turtle's natural instincts, encouraging it to explore its surroundings and problem-solve. By using objects to create small "rivers" or pathways, you can add variety and complexity to your turtle's habitat. This kind of environmental enrichment helps your turtle stay active, both mentally and physically.

If your turtle goes through brumation during the colder months, it's important to continue monitoring its health during this period. Brumation, which is similar to hibernation, is a time when your turtle's activity level decreases, and there is less opportunity for mental stimulation. During brumation, make sure to check on your turtle periodically to ensure that it is healthy and not stressed. Even though it's in a dormant state, the environment should still be kept clean and safe.

Once brumation ends, it's important to reintroduce enrichment activities gradually. This helps your turtle transition back into its normal routine. After a period of dormancy, your turtle might be sluggish or less active at first, so start by providing simpler stimulation, like food puzzles or gently rearranging the environment. Gradually increase the challenges and activities as your turtle becomes more active and engaged.

Chapter 14

ADDRESSING PICKY EATERS

S potted turtles, like many other reptiles, can sometimes be picky eaters. In captivity, they may refuse certain foods or show little interest in eating at all. While this can be frustrating, it's important to understand why this happens and what you can do to encourage your turtle to eat a balanced diet.

One common reason for picky eating is stress or illness. Stress can occur if there are sudden changes in your turtle's environment, such as a new enclosure setup, loud noises nearby, or the introduction of other animals. These changes can make your turtle anxious, leading to a decrease in appetite. Illness is another potential cause. Health problems like infections, parasites, or other conditions can make a turtle lose interest in food. If your turtle seems unusually quiet, weak, or inactive, illness could be the underlying issue.

Another reason for picky eating is dietary preference. Just like humans, turtles can have their own food likes and dislikes. For example, some spotted turtles might prefer live insects over vegetables or aquatic plants. While it's good to provide variety in their diet, it's natural for turtles to have preferences for certain foods over others.

If your turtle has become a picky eater, the first step is to check for stress or illness. Pay close attention to your turtle's behavior and health. Look for signs like lethargy, swelling, changes in the shell, or abnormal activity. If you notice anything unusual, consult a veterinarian who is experienced with reptiles to rule out any health problems. It's important to address any medical issues promptly, as they can significantly affect your turtle's appetite and overall well-being.

To help a picky turtle start eating again, try offering a wide variety of foods. In the wild, spotted turtles eat a mix of aquatic plants, insects, and small invertebrates. In captivity, you can mimic this natural diet by providing leafy greens like dandelion greens, kale, or collard greens. Offer live insects such as crickets, mealworms, or earthworms, as well as small fish. Experiment with different types of food to see what your turtle enjoys. You can also alternate between live food, fresh vegetables, and prepared commercial turtle diets to add variety and ensure they receive a balanced diet.

Sometimes making food more appealing can encourage your turtle to eat. For example, offer food at different times of the day to see when your turtle is most active and willing to eat. Using tongs to present food directly in front of your turtle can also help. Many turtles enjoy hunting their food, so live insects or moving food items may catch their interest. Presenting food in small, manageable pieces can also make it easier for them to eat.

It's also important to ensure that your turtle's habitat is set up correctly. Poor habitat conditions can contribute to picky eating. For example, turtles need the right temperature, lighting, and humidity to stay healthy and feel comfortable enough to eat. Make sure your turtle has a proper basking area where it can warm up, as basking helps with digestion. The water temperature should be maintained at the appropriate level, and the enclosure should have good water quality. Clean, fresh water is essential for both hydration and overall health. If these environmental factors are not ideal, your turtle may become stressed, which can affect its appetite.

MANAGING AGGRESSION OR TERRITORIAL BEHAVIOR

Spotted turtles are generally calm and solitary in the wild, but they can sometimes show aggression or territorial behavior in captivity. These behaviors might occur if a turtle feels that its space is being invaded or if there is competition for resources. Aggression can lead to stress or injury, so it's important to manage these behaviors to keep your turtles safe and comfortable.

One of the main causes of aggression is overcrowding. Turtles are territorial by nature, and when too many turtles are kept in one enclosure, they may compete for space, food, and basking spots. This competition can lead to fights or dominance displays. Overcrowding can also make turtles feel stressed or unsafe, which might make them act aggressively toward each other.

Another common cause of aggression is mating season. During this time, male turtles may become more aggressive as they compete for the attention of females. They may chase or nip at each other or at the females. Females can also become territorial during nesting season, especially if they feel that they don't have enough space or privacy to lay their eggs.

Competition for resources is another reason for aggressive behavior. If turtles don't have enough food, basking spots, or hiding places, they may fight over these limited resources. For example, if there is only one basking spot in the enclosure, turtles may push each other off it or prevent others from using it. Limited food can also cause disputes, as turtles may feel the need to defend their share.

To manage aggression or territorial behavior, the first step is to make sure your turtles have enough space. A larger enclosure can give each turtle the room it needs to feel secure. When turtles have enough space to move around and establish their own territories, they are less likely to fight. As a general rule, each turtle should have enough room to swim, bask, and hide without constantly encountering others.

It's also important to monitor how your turtles interact with each other. If you notice signs of aggression, such as biting, chasing, or constant fighting, consider separating the turtles. Some turtles simply don't get along with others, and it may be better to house them in separate enclosures. This is especially important if one turtle is consistently aggressive and causing harm to others.

Another way to reduce aggression is to ensure that there are plenty of resources for all the turtles. For example, if you have multiple turtles, provide multiple basking spots so that each one has its own place to rest. Add extra hiding places, such as logs, rocks, or plants, so turtles can retreat when they need privacy. When feeding your turtles, spread the food out in different areas of the enclosure to prevent them from fighting over it. This helps to reduce competition and keeps the environment more peaceful.

If aggression is linked to mating season, be prepared for increased territorial behavior during this time. Male turtles may need to be separated to prevent fighting, and females should have a quiet, private space for nesting. You can create a nesting area with soft, sandy soil where females can dig and lay their eggs without being disturbed. Once the mating season is over, the turtles may return to their calmer behavior.

In cases where one turtle is particularly aggressive, it may be best to keep that turtle in its own enclosure. Some turtles have dominant personalities and do not tolerate living with others, no matter how much space or how many resources are provided. Separating the aggressive turtle can help create a calmer and safer environment for the other turtles.

COPING WITH ENVIRONMENTAL CHANGES

Spotted turtles are very sensitive to changes in their environment. Any sudden changes, whether in temperature, water quality, or lighting, can cause them stress. Stress in turtles can lead to changes in their behavior and even health problems. It's important to carefully manage their environment to ensure they stay happy and healthy.

One common environmental change that can affect spotted turtles is fluctuations in temperature. Turtles are cold-blooded animals, which means they rely on their environment to maintain their body temperature. If their enclosure gets too hot or too cold, it can cause them stress and even make them sick. For example, if the water temperature drops too low, a turtle may become sluggish, stop eating, or even develop respiratory infections. Similarly, if the basking area gets too hot, the turtle may overheat and become dehydrated.

Water quality is another critical factor. Since spotted turtles spend much of their time in water, keeping the water clean is very important. If the water becomes dirty or its pH changes, it can cause serious health problems like shell rot or skin infections. Poor water quality can also make the turtle feel stressed and uncomfortable, especially if there is too much ammonia or if the water temperature is not ideal.

Lighting changes can also affect spotted turtles. Turtles need the right amount of light to stay healthy. They require UVB lighting to help their bodies produce vitamin D3, which is essential for their shells and bones. A sudden change in lighting can disrupt their natural rhythms, including their eating and sleeping patterns. If they don't get enough light, they may become lethargic or develop health problems over time.

To help spotted turtles cope with these environmental changes, there are several steps you can take. First, always maintain stable temperatures in their enclosure. Use heaters and thermostats to keep the water temperature between 75-80°F (24-27°C) and the basking area between 85-90°F (29-32°C). Check these temperatures regularly to ensure there are no sudden drops or spikes. Sudden changes in temperature can stress the turtle and make it more vulnerable to illness.

Second, take care of water quality by using a good filtration system to keep the water clean. You should test the water regularly to check its pH, ammonia levels, and temperature. A good pH level for turtles is usually around 6.5 to 7.5. Change the water frequently to ensure it stays fresh, and provide shallow areas where your turtle can easily access clean water to drink.

Third, provide proper lighting in the enclosure. Spotted turtles need UVB light for about 10-12 hours each day to stay healthy. UVB light helps their bodies produce vitamin D3, which they need to process calcium and maintain strong shells and bones. You should also mimic a natural day-night cycle by ensuring the enclosure is dark for 12-14 hours each night. Avoid changing the lighting schedule suddenly, as this can disrupt their sleep and behavior.

When introducing new elements to the turtle's enclosure, make changes gradually. For example, if you add new plants, decorations, or tank mates, introduce them slowly so the turtle has time to adjust. A sudden change in their surroundings can cause stress, so it's best to let them explore and get used to new items over time.

Chapter 15

THE LIFESPAN OF SPOTTED TURTLES

Spotted turtles are known for their long lifespan, making them a special and rewarding pet for those who are prepared for a long-term commitment. On average, a spotted turtle can live between 25 and 50 years, but some individuals have been known to live even longer. With the right care, these turtles can thrive for decades, making them a pet that may be with you for much of your life.

One of the most important factors in determining how long a spotted turtle will live is the level of care it receives. Proper care includes creating and maintaining a suitable environment that meets all its needs. For example, the turtle's enclosure must be clean and well-maintained. This means regularly cleaning the water and substrate to prevent the build-up of harmful bacteria or waste. The enclosure should also mimic the turtle's natural habitat as closely as possible, providing areas for swimming, basking, and hiding. Consistent water quality, appropriate temperatures, and access to UVB lighting are essential for their health and can have a direct impact on their lifespan.

A balanced diet is another critical factor in helping your turtle live a long and healthy life. Spotted turtles eat a mix of aquatic plants, insects, and small invertebrates in the wild. In captivity, their diet should include a variety of nutritious foods such as leafy greens, insects, and commercial turtle pellets designed to provide all the vitamins and minerals they need. Calcium is particularly important for maintaining a healthy shell and bones. You can provide calcium by dusting their food with a calcium supplement or offering cuttlebone in their enclosure. Providing a well-rounded diet helps prevent nutritional deficiencies that could lead to health problems and a shortened lifespan.

Genetics also play a role in a spotted turtle's lifespan. A turtle that comes from healthy parents and has no genetic issues is more likely to live a long and healthy life. If you are purchasing a spotted turtle, choose one from a reputable breeder or adopt one from a rescue. Reputable breeders ensure their turtles are healthy and free from hereditary issues. Adopting from a rescue is another great option, as many rescues conduct health checks on turtles before placing them with new owners. Starting with a healthy turtle gives it the best chance of living a long life.

In addition to providing proper care and ensuring good genetics, regular health monitoring is crucial. Spotted turtles, like all animals, can develop health issues over time. By observing your turtle closely, you can catch potential problems early. Watch for signs of illness, such as a loss of appetite, lethargy, unusual behavior, or changes in the appearance of the shell or skin. If you notice anything unusual, consult a veterinarian who specializes in reptiles. Regular check-ups with a reptile vet can also help identify and address issues before they become serious. Preventative care, such as keeping the enclosure clean and meeting all the turtle's needs, reduces the risk of common health problems.

It's important to understand that owning a spotted turtle is a long-term commitment. Because these turtles live for several decades, caring for one means being prepared to provide for its needs for a significant portion of your life. This includes daily tasks like feeding and cleaning, as well as planning for their care as they age. Additionally, you should think about what will happen if your circumstances change. For example, if you can no longer care for the turtle due to relocation, health reasons, or other life changes, it's important to have a plan in place. Arranging for a trusted friend, family member, or another responsible person to take over their care ensures the turtle's well-being even if you are no longer able to look after it.

BUILDING A ROUTINE FOR PROPER CARE

Establishing a regular care routine is essential for keeping your spotted turtle healthy and happy. A predictable schedule helps reduce stress, ensures your turtle's needs are consistently met, and allows you to notice any changes in its behavior or health early. Below is a simple guide to creating and maintaining a routine for your turtle's care.

Daily care is the foundation of your routine. Feeding your turtle regularly is crucial for its health. Younger turtles, such as hatchlings and juveniles, need to eat daily or every other day, as they are growing quickly. Adult turtles, on the other hand, can be fed every two to three days. Offer a balanced diet that includes leafy greens, insects, and turtle pellets. Be sure to remove any leftover food after feeding to prevent it from spoiling and contaminating the water.

It's also important to observe your turtle every day. Pay attention to its activity level and behavior. A healthy turtle will be alert and move around its enclosure. If you notice signs of illness, such as a lack of appetite, unusual behavior, or changes in the shell's appearance, take action immediately. These could be signs of stress or a health problem that needs attention.

If your turtle's enclosure includes a water section, make it a habit to check the water quality daily. Remove any debris, uneaten food, or waste to keep the water clean and safe. Clean water helps prevent health issues like shell infections or respiratory problems.

Weekly care tasks help keep your turtle's habitat clean and well-maintained. Spot-clean the enclosure daily, but set aside time each week for a more thorough cleaning. This includes scrubbing algae off surfaces, replacing any soiled substrate, and refreshing the water in the tank or pond. Maintaining a clean habitat is key to your turtle's long-term health.

Check the temperature and lighting weekly as well. Spotted turtles need a basking area with a temperature between 85-90°F (29-32°C) and water that is around 75-80°F (24-27°C). They also require UVB lighting to stay healthy. Make sure the bulbs are working properly and replace them as needed. UVB bulbs lose their effectiveness over time, even if they still produce light, so replace them every six months to a year.

Monthly and seasonal care tasks go beyond daily and weekly responsibilities to ensure your turtle stays in good condition. Once a month, take a closer look at your turtle's overall health. Examine its shell for any signs of damage, such as cracks or discoloration, and monitor its weight to track its growth. Weighing your turtle regularly helps you identify potential health problems early, such as weight loss or poor appetite.

If your turtle brumates (hibernates) during the winter, prepare its habitat for this period of dormancy. Lower the temperature gradually, and make sure the water and environment are clean and safe for brumation. After the brumation period is over, slowly adjust the habitat back to its normal temperature and light levels to ease your turtle back into its regular routine.

Enrichment is also an important part of your turtle's care. Rotate decorations, hiding spots, and plants in the enclosure to provide new experiences for your turtle. This keeps it mentally stimulated and prevents boredom, which can lead to stress.

Long-term planning is another key part of caring for a spotted turtle, as these animals can live for decades. Regular checkups with a reptile veterinarian are essential for preventative care. Even if your turtle appears healthy, a vet can identify potential issues before they become serious. This helps ensure that your turtle has a long and healthy life.

Caring for a turtle over many years can be expensive. Food, habitat upgrades, lighting, and medical care all come with costs. Plan your budget to cover these expenses so you can provide the best care for your turtle without financial stress.

Finally, since spotted turtles can live for 25-50 years or more, it's important to think about their future care. If something happens and you are no longer able to care for your turtle, have a plan in place. Identify a trusted family member, friend, or rescue organization that can take responsibility for your turtle if needed. This ensures your pet will be cared for even if your circumstances change.

Made in United States
Troutdale, OR
01/23/2025

28215194R00046